What Are They Saying About Euthanasia?

Richard M. Gula, S.S.

PAULIST PRESS
New York/Mahwah

Library of Congress
Catalog Card Number: 85-62879

ISBN: 0-8091-2766-0

Published by Paulist Press
997 Macarthur Boulevard
Mahwah, N.J. 07430

Printed and bound in the
United States of America

Contents

Introduction

Should medicine do all that it can? This is one of the principal questions for medical ethics, and whether to administer or to forego life-prolonging treatment is a specification of that general question. It is one of the greatest dilemmas modern medicine faces.

A patient, sedated and comatose, or nearly so, tethered by tubes to an array of machinery, is the familiar example of institutional dying in our high-tech medical facilities. What is the best care for a patient in such a condition? What is the moral balance between preserving life and preventing suffering? Should life be preserved regardless of the circumstances? Should those who are not dying but whose lives will be seriously impaired, like some handicapped newborns or victims of spinal cord injuries, be given treatment at all? Can patients like these be allowed to die without life-saving interventions and machinery? Is it ever permissible to intervene directly, but mercifully, to hasten death when death is inevitable and the dying process is so anguishing? The ethical issues surrounding the care and treatment of terminally ill patients, as well as those who are not dying but whose lives will linger with serious debilitation, are receiving more attention as medicine's capacity to prolong life increases.

Many factors have propelled the moral responsibility of prolonging life to center stage. The union of medicine and technology is a leading one, and has caused some confusing consequences. For example, the same technology which extends the life of one person may simply prolong the dying of another. Also, medical use of technology has produced new options for the qual-

1

ity of our lives. We now have for many life-threatening conditions some form of medical intervention which can delay the moment of death and add more days, weeks, months, or even years to a person's life. Since so many deaths in America occur in hospitals or extended care facilities, health care professionals often have ready access to the technology which adds length of days to life. But the technology which postpones death does not necessarily secure a tolerable state of well-being so that living longer would mean really living better. More and more, people are concerned about the quality of the lives saved by technology. Unless we are merely willing to let the presence of technology "compel" us to use it, we must make some hard choices about using these techniques. The availability of the technology, in fact, allows death to be more a matter of decision than a matter of chance.

Likewise, an increasing number of movies, plays, books, talk shows, news broadcasts and documentaries have heightened public awareness that efforts to prolong life can become, unintentionally, a means to prolong dying. As a result of the disturbing pictorial sight of dying people hooked up to machines, together with the public discussion of mechanically sustaining the life of those who are irreversibly unconscious, many do not fear death as much as they fear lingering in a seriously debilitated condition without the relief of either restored health or death. More and more people are beginning to recognize that life is not an absolute good and that death is not an absolute evil. In fact, questions pertaining to the moral responsibility of prolonging life are being considered in an atmosphere where death is being re-evaluated as a potential good and not in an atmosphere where life is considered as necessarily to be sustained at all costs.

The plight of Karen Ann Quinlan has also brought the problem of care for the dying to center stage. She has become the classic example of technologically prolonged dying. On April 15, 1975 she stopped breathing. Although resuscitation efforts restored breathing, Karen Ann remained comatose, a victim of irreversible brain damage. Thirteen months after Karen Ann had lapsed into a coma, and after months of litigation to win the sanction of the New Jersey Supreme Court to remove the respirator without legal jeopardy, the respirator was removed but Karen Ann did not die. (She remained in a coma for over ten years until she died on June 11, 1985 of respiratory failure following acute pneumonia.) Before the Quinlan case in 1975, the public discussion of the right to die or of the definition of death was meager. Since then, however, the discussion has widened to include not only physicians but also jurists, philosophers, theologians and the public at large.

Two types of problems have kept before the public the subject of appropriate care for the dying. One type has to do with dying patients being overtreated. Court cases like those of Karen Ann Quinlan and Br. Joseph Fox which involved the use of a respirator on irreversibly comatose patients, or that of Joseph Saikewicz which involved the use of chemotherapy to treat a sixty-seven year old mentally retarded man with acute leukemia, and that of Earl Spring which involved the use of dialysis on a seventy-seven year old senile man represent cases disputing whether too many medical technologies were being used.

The other type of case has to do with patients being undertreated. The court case of Clarence Herbert which involved the withdrawal of all life-support systems including nutrition and fluids from a patient who was clinically diagnosed as clearly dying is such an example. The courts judged in favor of the decision to withdraw his life-supports. Another type of case pertains to withholding or withdrawing life-supportive means, including nutrition and fluids, from patients who are not clearly dying but who are living and will probably continue to live with some degree of debilitation. Examples of these are the case of Baby Doe of Bloomington which involved corrective surgery for tracheo-esophageal fistula on a Down's Syndrome infant, and the case of Claire Conroy, an eighty-four year old senile, gravely ill woman in a New Jersey nursing home, who needed artificial feeding to survive. The courts did not intervene against the decision to let the baby die, but the courts did intervene to require that Claire Conroy be fed. Later, the Supreme Court of New Jersey reversed this decision. However, by that time Miss Conroy had already died with her feeding tubes intact. These cases represent disputes as to whether enough care was being given.

Also, in recent years we have experienced the efforts of the Euthanasia Educational Council, now known as "Concern for Dying," to promote the "living will"—a document that allows a patient to give a physician informed consent, in advance of a terminal illness or after it has begun, to end medical treatment and to allow the patient to die without life-sustaining equipment. Closely following upon the popularity of living wills came legislative efforts to enact "natural death" acts (California being the pioneer in this movement with its 1976 legislation) to give legal status to the living will concept. More recently, the rapid advance of durable power of attorney for health care statutes in many states is providing a simpler and more flexible legal mechanism than either the living will or natural death acts for making decisions for patients lacking the mental capacity to do so. Another sign of public and political interest in ethical issues created by the technical advances in medicine is the establishment by Congress in 1978 of the President's Commission for the Study of Ethical Problems in Medicine and Biomedical and Behavioral Research. This commission was dissolved after the completion of its work and the publication of its reports. This is unfortunate since ongoing study by a commission of this nature would be very helpful in these times of rapid advance in the biological and behavioral science research fields.

Factors like these have created a forum in which discussions about dying and death are taking place. As a result, many more people, not just health care professionals, are talking more openly about dying and death. These once taboo subjects seem to be stealing the limelight from sex. Questions about sustaining life, about dying and about death are part of public dialogue. Shall a person suffering a terminal illness be given life-sustaining treatment? Is there a moral difference between not starting a respirator and turning it off once it is on? Is it permissible to relieve pain with drugs which inevitably hasten death? Can a patient morally refuse life-prolonging treatment? When is a person dead? How can we care for the dying so as to uphold personal dignity? Is it ever permissible to hurry death along by directly intervening in the dying process? These are some of the many questions being raised in the public debates which open us to ethical considerations of terminal care and which draw us into the discussion of euthanasia.

This book will try to bring into focus the complex discussion of euthanasia which is marked by significant diversity, incompleteness, tentativeness, and probing strategies. We will meet many difficulties in trying to discuss euthanasia in a disciplined way, not the least of which is the term "euthanasia" with its troubling ambiguities. As a concept, "euthanasia" is not used in a uniform way. Originally meaning a good or happy death, "euthanasia" has acquired a connotation of violence or evil, making it synonymous with murder and a social policy of killing those suffering from incurable disease, old age or a serious physical handicap. Recently, the Hemlock Society has tried to rehabilitate the positive sense of euthanasia by encouraging voluntary easy deaths.

The ambiguity of "euthanasia" and the moral repugnance of its negative connotations have given rise to other terms which try to do justice to the different ways of meeting death swiftly but painlessly. "Mercy killing" may be the most popular alternative. Others are "agathanasia," "anti-dysthanasia" and "benemortasia." None of these alternatives have succeeded in winning a consensus.

Often, however, we find "euthanasia" with a qualifier. "Active" (also positive or direct) euthanasia, also known as "mercy killing" or "causing to die," designates someone's doing something to another with the intention of shortening that person's life. If this is done to persons with their consent, it is called "voluntary euthanasia." If it is done without their consent, it is called "non-voluntary active euthanasia." Legally, active euthanasia is considered homicide. "Passive" (also negative or indirect) euthanasia is also known as "allowing to die." It designates the removing or withholding of life-supporting means, such as antibiotics, transfusions, respirators, dialysis and the like, because no reasonable hope of recovery exists for the dying person. This can also be voluntary or non-voluntary depending on whether consent is given or not. Sometimes "natural death" or "death with dignity" is used in place of "voluntary passive euthanasia." Some states have given legal recognition to passive euthanasia in legislation which recognizes the right to refuse treatment. California was the first to do so with its Natural Death Act in 1976. Durable power of attorney for health care statutes do the same thing in a simpler and more flexible way.

This book cannot resolve the terminological problem with its related philosophical issues, but, recognizing the complexity, this book will focus primarily on the moral principles, issues and positions which have occupied the euthanasia discussion in the recent past.[1] Like other books in this series, this is a work of exposition. It brings diverse views together for comparison. The result is not a perfect blending that produces a new super-theory, but a clarifying of the directions of the current discussion on this subject. Hopefully, this will contribute to a deepened and enriched view of a number of perspectives that should be seen together. The literature on this subject is enormous. As a result, this book cannot hope to represent what everyone is saying about euthanasia, but it does try to represent those who have made a significant contribution primarily to the discussion of the moral issues pertaining to euthanasia.

In order to bring some focus to the discussion, I will address five primary questions. (1) What is death and when may a person be declared dead? These questions engage the philosophical issue of defining death as well as the medical criteria for determining death and the trends in death legislation. (2) What are some of the fundamental issues in the discussion of euthanasia? This question opens us to the various ways of interpreting the principles of sanctity of life, dominion over life and human stewardship, as well as interpreting the difference between commission and omission, and the moral meaning of ordinary and extraordinary means of treatment. (3) What are some of the leading positions being proposed on euthanasia? In response to this question, I will explore ten positions which represent the spectrum of the contemporary discussion. (4) Practically, what is the nature of our responsibility to care for the terminally ill? This considers the practical issues of who should decide what will be done, of telling the truth to the dying patient, and of the hospice concept of caring for the terminally ill. (5) Succinctly, what is the moral art of terminal care? This presents an integrated view fashioned on the basis of the fundamental moral convictions which ought to shape our vision and action when caring for the terminally ill.

I owe debts of gratitude to several individuals who spent considerable time reading this book and providing me with criticisms and observations. For this I am grateful to my Sulpician colleagues, Frs. Gerald D. Coleman, S.S. and Philip S. Keane, S.S., as well as to Albert R. Jonsen, Professor of Ethics in Medicine in the Department of Medicine at the School of Medicine of the University of California, San Francisco. I am also grateful to Fr. Steve Rowan for his valuable time and talent as proofreader and for his suggestions for making this book more readable. A final word of thanks goes to my dad whose living and dying has taught me the art of loving with gentleness and care. This book is dedicated to him.

1
Determining Death

Dead or alive. What could be simpler? Yet determining death is not as simple as it may seem. Even defining death is not easy. Traditionally, when the heart stopped beating and the lungs stopped breathing, we regarded the person dead. Medical technology has changed that. The biomedical revolution of the past few decades permits us to treat the body organ by organ. For example, breathing, blood circulation, taking nourishment, and eliminating waste can be sustained artificially for prolonged periods of time even while the brain is totally or near totally destroyed. Is a patient in such a condition dead? Conditions like these have forced us to re-examine our accepted standard for determining death—namely, the cessation of respiration and circulation.

Before taking up a discussion of the issues and positions on euthanasia, we need to distinguish the issue of euthanasia from a different, though related issue—determining the moment of death. After all, the morality of euthanasia is concerned with the obligations and limits of keeping the person alive. If the person is clearly dead, we no longer have to consider the obligation to prolong life. But if the person is even probably alive, then we do have to consider this obligation. Before we can discuss euthanasia as a moral issue, then, we have to know whether the person is dead or alive. How is that determined?

The need to determine death clearly and precisely has some solid pragmatic grounds. For example, the use of mechanical means of life-support raises problems for the familiar heart-lung criteria for determining death. If we were able to declare a patient dead in a situation where the heart and lungs are being sustained artificially after the brain has deteriorated beyond the point of returning to consciousness, then we could relieve the burden of emotional exhaustion of both family and health care staff. We could also relieve the financial burden entailed in prolonging futile treatment, and we could enable patients who have reversible conditions to have access to intensive care resources. Moreover, the increasing use of organ transplants, which require that an organ be removed as soon as possible once a person has died, also force a re-examination of the criteria of death. Criteria for determining death which have the support of law would protect transplant surgeons against suits of wrongful death.

Each of these reasons is based on the pragmatic benefit that a common definition and agreed upon criteria of death would bring to others. However, Robert Veatch has rightly suggested that another reason is morally primary. This reason is that a person who is alive ought not to be treated as though he or she were dead.[1] Until death can be clearly affirmed, a patient retains all human rights and must be treated with the respect due the living, even though he or she may be dying. We preserve human dignity by being able to distinguish the dead from the living. We ought to render appropriate care to the living, but once death occurs we would offend human dignity if we did not replace artificial life-support means with behavior more befitting a patient who has died.

The accepted standard for determining death has been the cardiopulmonary criteria of the irreversible cessation of respiration and circulation. But now biomedical technology is able to generate breathing and heartbeat when these spontaneous functions break down. The presence of such mechanical life-supports makes determining the death of the human person as a whole more urgent. This determination involves a complex interaction between technical aspects of medical diagnosis and the philosophical and theological considerations which underlie the judgment that a human organism in a particular situation is dead. Legal dimensions are also relevant to determining death.

Recently, some states have enacted death legislation to protect the living and the dead. This chapter will explore some of the issues related to the philosophical, theological, medical and legal dimensions of determining death.

Philosophical and Theological Dimensions of Determining Death

Discussions of determining death often confuse three issues: a philosophical or theological concept of death, empirical/physiological criteria for determining death, and clinical tests to show that the criteria are fulfilled. But the concept of death exists on a different plane than do the criteria and tests. These latter are properly empirical tasks; the former is not. However, the confidence we place in the empirical tasks depends on the role we allow for them in our concept of death.

At present, no universal formal definition of death has emerged from the discussion of the determination of death.[2] We do have general agreement that death marks the loss of what is essentially significant to human life. But unless this "significance" can be satisfactorily formulated, no one can finally decide what medical criteria can appropriately measure it. The medical certification of death ultimately presupposes a philosophical or theological concept of death. Biological criteria and medical tests merely verify that the concept applies in a certain case.

Robert Veatch has been highly influential in this discussion. He identifies four "concepts" of death as competing in the determination of death discussion: heart-lung death, death as the separation of soul and body, whole brain death, and cerebral death.[3] Each of these "concepts" implies that human life involves some interconnectedness of various aspects of the human person and that death results when this interconnectedness breaks down. However, these "concepts" cannot be treated as though they exist on the same plane. The philosophical/theological concept of the separation of soul and body does not share the empirical/physiological plane of the other three. These other three are unified by appealing to empirical criteria. They are more properly seen as signs certifying that the philosophical/theological concept of death has been fulfilled.

Theologically speaking, death means that a person has lost the capacity to receive God's gift of life. When a person's receptive capacity for this gift ceases, then the mode of human life ends and a new mode begins. The classical theological formula for death has been "the separation of body and soul." Karl Rahner has argued that this formula is limited as a way to understand death.[4] He regards it as little more than a description of death, and not as an essential definition. Rahner does not regard it as a definition of death since it speaks only of death as a physical fact and not as a personal, human event. It fails to account for what happens to the human being as a whole being and as a spiritual person. The formula says nothing about the specifically human factor of death being the free, personal self-realization before God. Another limitation is that it leaves the concept of separation obscure. What happens to the soul? From the theological point of view, this formula says that in death the soul assumes a new and different relation to the body. A dualistic anthropology would assume that at death the soul loses all relation to the body or the material world. Rahner's use of the hylomorphic theory, however, has challenged such a view by arguing that at death the soul retains a new and different relationship to the body and the material world. Since the soul is no longer bound to an individual bodily structure, it becomes more intimately related to the unity of the whole universe.

With this formulation of a concept of death, practical problems of determining the moment of death remain. For example, how can anyone determine when the soul has separated from the body? Are not biological criteria such as those applied to the heart-lung and brain concepts of death necessary for this determination? In dealing with the question of when death takes place, Pius XII clearly acknowledged that the Church lacks the competence to determine the moment of death:

> Where the verification of the fact [of death] in particular cases is concerned, the answer cannot be deduced from any religious

and moral principle and, under this aspect, does not fall within the competence of the Church.[5]

Rahner also recognizes the limits of theological competence. In determining the moment of death, he says, the theologian needs the help of biology. To arrive at a judgment of the moment of death, the theologian depends on biology even though the essentially theological statement of what constitutes human death is unaffected by the developments of the biological sciences.[6]

The theological understanding of death is not incompatible with using neurological or cardiopulmonary criteria to establish the time of death. The value of speaking of death as the separation of body and soul is that it does show that human life and death cannot be explained exhaustively in organic terms without some personal, spiritual principle. Furthermore, even though this theological notion does not provide empirical criteria for determining death, it does indicate the question we need to ask about death, namely, "*When* does the inner unity of the person cease?" To answer this question, we need empirical criteria. This brings us to the second level of the discussion over determining death—the medical dimensions.

Medical Dimensions of Determining Death

The medical level of the discussion is interested in criteria and tests to apply to bodily functions and structures to determine whether the patient is alive or dead. Ultimately, the certification that the patient is "dead" is not just a matter of scientific evidence. The scientific evidence can give a description of the condition of the person. But whether this condition represents a loss of that which is essentially significant to being human is ultimately a philosophical or theological judgment, not a medical one. Therefore, the concept of death determines the status of the medical criteria.

The heart-lung determination of death attends to the circulatory and respiratory organs and systems to determine death. The irreversible loss of spontaneous heart and lung functions is the clinical sign of death. This loss can be tested by simple observations—listening for a heartbeat, feeling the pulse, or seeing respiration—or by technical means through the use of an electrocardiogram or by measuring blood gases.

In most cases, the circulatory and respiratory criteria are sufficient to determine death. But in those instances of a patient's being supported by a mechanical respirator which can keep blood and oxygen circulating, the heart-lung criteria for death are no longer useful. The mechanical respirator delays the deterioration of the vital organs of the circulatory and respiratory system even after the neurological unity of the human organism ceases. For this reason, in instances of artificially sustained heart and lung action, relying on the heart-lung oriented criteria alone can give a false diagnosis of life. Other clinical signs of death are necessary. This is especially important in cases of prospective organ transplants. How is it possible to be sure that the donor is in fact dead when mechanical means are sustaining heart and lung action?

The possibility of a false diagnosis of life coming from the traditional cardiovascular criteria has forced the development of brain-oriented criteria of death. However, since the loss of respiratory and cardiac function will inevitably destroy the brain, the heart-lung criteria are reliable determinations of death and can serve as short-cuts for determining death in most cases. Only when the heart-lung criteria cannot be used are the brain-oriented criteria especially necessary.

The whole brain determination of death looks to the cerebrum (with its outer shell called the cortex), the cerebellum, and the brainstem (composed of the midbrain, the pons, and the medulla oblongata) to determine death. These are the parts of the brain which regulate the capacity for bodily integration. The medical profession seems to have adopted whole brain death as the way to determine human death in the extraordinary cases and implicitly, at least, in the ordinary cases. This is because the loss of spontaneous circulation and respiration is due to the loss of brainstem function.

Whole brain death rests on a philosophical view of personal integration, for it takes into consideration the vitality of the person as an integrated whole. It is not limited to the vitality of just one or two organs taken independently of the whole. Neurological integration of the body's physiological system is necessary. Without the whole brain functioning, the individual is able to integrate neither his or her internal bodily environment (an unconscious operation) nor social environment through consciousness. Even though metabolism may continue in some cells and organs, the person is not properly regarded as alive when the body's physiological system ceases to function as an integrated whole. Whole brain death is an improvement over the cardiorespiratory determination of death because it shows that breathing and circulation are necessary though not sufficient to establish that a person is alive.

This is the concept of death that has received increasing favor among some philosophers and theologians. For example, philosophers Charles M. Culver and Bernard Gert, for whom death is strictly a biological concept, define death as the "permanent cessation of functioning of the organism as a whole."[7] For them, the permanent loss of functioning of the entire brain correlates with the cessation of functioning of the organism as a whole. Among theologians, Charles J. McFadden, a Roman Catholic moral theologian instrumental in contributing to the emergence of Catholic medical ethics in this country, accepts the whole brain concept of death. "Once the fact of brain death has been established," he writes, "*the person is dead,* even though heartbeat and respiration are continued by mechanical means."[8] Bernard Häring, the prominent Roman Catholic moral theologian instrumental in Catholic efforts to rethink moral theology in light of the biblical and scientific revolutions of recent decades, accepts whole brain death also: "Personally, I feel that the arguments for the equation of the total death of the person with brain death are fully valid."[9] Paul Ramsey, a prominent Protestant ethician, does not oppose the brain death concept though he does oppose using this concept of death solely to enhance prospects of acquiring fresh organs from a prospective donor for the purposes of a transplant. Ramsey's hope is that updating the concept of death to brain death "would be so *that* persons who have died need not have 'life' sustaining measures inflicted upon their unburied corpses, needlessly and at great expense to their families."[10] The President's Commission report, *Defining Death,* has also adopted this whole brain standard of death. In the commission's words, "death is that moment at which the body's physiological system ceases to constitute an integrated whole."[11]

While the concept of whole brain death seems to be generally accepted in the medical profession, the specific criteria used to determine it have not been agreed upon by all. However, the set of criteria which seem to have attracted the widest attention and have received substantial approval are those which are popularly known as the "Harvard criteria." In 1968 the first serious attempt to develop a set of empirical criteria indicating irreversible loss of whole brain activity was carried out by the Ad Hoc Committee of the Harvard Medical School to Examine the Definition of Brain Death.[12] These criteria describe the characteristics of an irreversible coma and are the ones most widely recognized to determine brain death. The Harvard criteria are these:

1. *Unreceptivity and Unresponsitivity*
   This means the patient is totally unaware and unresponsive to externally applied stimuli. Even very painful stimuli do not evoke a vocal response of any sort, nor limb withdrawal.

2. *No Movements or Breathing*
   This means that during the period of at least an hour, the patient shows no signs of spontaneous muscular movement, breathing, or response to stimuli of any sort.

3. *No Reflexes*
   The surest sign of the absence of reflex action is the fixed, dilated pupil. Other reflex centers also show no response.

4. *Flat Electroencephalogram*
   The flat EEG, implying an absence of biological activity of the brain cells, confirms the other criteria and should be used when available.

All these tests are to be repeated twenty-four hours later. No change in the results confirms whole brain death. The validity of the data as indications of whole brain death depends on excluding two conditions: hypothermia (body temperature below 90° F) or central nervous system depressants, such as barbiturates.

The certitude of the Harvard criteria for diagnosing whole brain death was challenged along their way to becoming widely accepted as reliable criteria. For example, Adrienne Van Till, formal legal secretary of the Ad Hoc Committee on Organ Transplantation which the Netherlands Red Cross Society established in 1968, objects on the grounds that a flat EEG measures the activity of the cortex but does not give reliable information about deeper parts of the brain. According to Van Till, the flat EEG needs to be confirmed by angiography, a more decisive indicator, which tests cerebral blood flow.[13]

Another dissenting opinion comes from Byrne, Quay and O'Reilly who object on the grounds of the difference between a loss of brain function, which the Harvard criteria indicate, and total brain destruction which they propose. They argue that the absence of brain function may simply indicate a dormant condition of a still live brain. But these men propose no criteria for determining complete brain destruction over inactivity.[14] Moreover, "destruction" is ambiguous. Does it mean irreversible cessation of all activity? Or is it the anatomical destruction of brain tissue? Anatomical destruction is not ordinarily used to determine death, whereas the loss of function seems universally accepted.[15]

A 1970 study of the American Electroencephalographic Society showed that only three of 2,642 patients survived who had a flat EEG. These three survivors were drug overdose cases and so would fail to meet all the standards of the Harvard criteria.[16] Such evidence seems to confirm the validity of the reliability of the EEG and the Harvard criteria with as much certainty as possible in biology and medicine without the need to seek more conservative tests. Supplementary tests for blood flow to the brain, such as angiography, are purely optional when sufficient cause has already been established that the brain has ceased to function.[17] The medical consultants to the President's Commission report, *Defining Death,* have proposed an updated version of the "Harvard criteria" in light of the clinical experience accumulated since the original Harvard report in 1968. The medical consultants' "Guidelines" rely on clinical signs of absent cerebral and brain functions. The EEG is no longer necessary as a test though some medical circumstances may require its use to confirm clinical findings.[18]

However, Robert Veatch argues for determining death by focusing on cerebral death or the cessation of "higher brain" functions, such as thought, consciousness, memory, feeling, speech, and social interaction. The cerebrum regulates these "higher brain" functions which make humans different from, or superior to, animals or things. Veatch regards these complex activities of the higher brain centers (or of capacities to engage in them) to be essential attributes a human being must have to be a person. According to Veatch, cerebral death marks the loss of what is essential to a person. A breathing body, in other words, is not enough to be constituted a person. These higher brain centers can be destroyed while the "lower brain" continues to function, regulating reflex actions like eye movements, swallowing, yawning, and heart and lung functions. When the cerebrum is destroyed, the patient is in an irreversible coma and exists in what is usually called a "persistent vegetative state" or "persistent non-cognitive state" with no social interaction possible. Under the concept of cerebral death, a patient would be considered dead when cognition and consciousness are lost totally and social interaction becomes impossible, even though the heart and lungs continue to function spontaneously. Veatch points to the evidence which has been used to support the use of the EEG in the Harvard criteria as being persuasive enough to allow for using the EEG *alone* as empirical evidence of irreversible loss of neocortical function.[19]

The case of Karen Ann Quinlan has made the distinction between whole brain death and cerebral death familiar to the general public. While exhibiting involuntary movements like facial grimaces, yawning and blinking, Karen Ann's apparent wakefulness did not represent awareness of herself or her environment. With continued nursing care, feeding and antibiotics, she continued to survive without a respirator. Yet the implication of the cerebral death/personhood argument for determining death holds that Karen Quinlan was just as dead as a corpse in the traditional sense. However, no one advocated burying her in that condition as one would bury a corpse. Such reluctance shows a limitation of cerebral death and a general resistance to accept it as the sole determination of death. Cerebral death, however, does raise the question of whether continued life-support measures, such as antibiotics, nutrition and fluids, ought to continue to be used. We will look at this issue in the next chapter.

Legal Dimensions of Determining Death

Deciding which criteria to use as a matter of public policy brings us to the legal level of the discussion on determining death. Determination-of-death statutes could serve as a vehicle to translate a generally accepted medical standard into a form acceptable to most members of society. Hopefully this kind of legislation would minimize the burdens placed on both the family and the physicians of the dead patient.

Until quite recently the United States had no legal criteria for determining death. The common practice has been to accept the traditional criteria of heart-lung death. This is reflected in the definition of death found in *Black's Law Dictionary:*

> The cessation of life; the ceasing to exist; defined by physicians as a total stoppage of the circulation of the blood, and a cessation of the animal and vital functions consequent thereon, such as respiration, pulsation, etc. (1951, 4th edition).[20]

While this definition proved sufficient in most instances, the advent of artificial means of life-support to replace the functioning of heart and lungs has introduced severe limitations on this definition and its use in public policies. Furthermore, organ transplant procedures demand an accurate determination of death so that vital organs are not removed from the living, and transplant surgeons are not accused of homicide. Without social consensus on when death has occurred and legislation to reflect that consensus, the same human organism can be regarded as legally "dead" in one state but legally "alive" when the ambulance crosses the state line. Such a situation would result in variations in medical practice, public confusion, and different legal expectations of all parties.

Traditionally, standards for determining death have been a matter of state rather than federal law. This situation has given rise to variations among the laws of several states. Determination-of-death statutes fall into four categories.

1. Brain death is used as an alternative to the heart-lung determination of death.

This is found in the Kansas statute:

> A person will be considered medically and legally dead if, in the opinion of a physician, based on ordinary standards of medical practice, there is the absence of spontaneous respiration and cardiac function and, because of the disease or condition which caused, directly or indirectly, these functions to cease, or because of the passage of time since these functions ceased, attempts at resuscitation are considered hopeless; and, in this event, death will have occurred at the time these functions ceased; or

> A person will be considered medically and legally dead if, in the opinion of a physician, based on ordinary standards of medical practice, there is the absence of spontaneous brain function; and if based on ordinary standards of medical practice, during reasonable attempts to either maintain or restore spontaneous circulatory or respiratory function in the absence of aforesaid brain function, it appears that further attempts at resuscitation or supportive maintenance will not succeed, death will have occurred at the time when these conditions first coincide. Death is to be pronounced before any vital organ is removed for purposes of transplantation.

> These alternative definitions of death are to be utilized for all purposes in this state, including the trials of civil and criminal cases, any laws to the contrary notwithstanding.[21]

This statute has been criticized not only for implying two separate kinds of death, but also for not qualifying the meaning of "brain function." Furthermore, it remains open to abuse in cases of prospective organ transplants by allowing the donor to be considered dead at an earlier point in the dying process than an identical patient would be who was not a potential donor.[22]

2. Whole brain death is used as the alternative to the heart-lung determination of death.

This is found in the model legislation endorsed by the American Bar Association, the American Medical Association, the National Conference of Commissioners on Uniform State Laws, the American Academy of Neurology, the American Electroencephalographic Society, and the President's Commission:

> An individual who has sustained either (1) irreversible cessation of circulatory and respiratory functions, or (2) irreversible cessation of all functions of the entire brain, including the brain stem, is dead. A determination of death must be made in accordance with accepted medical standards.[23]

This statute has the advantage of being an improvement over the first model by qualifying "brain function" to mean "all functions of the entire brain, including the brain stem." With this qualification, this statute recognizes that death ensues when the body ceases to function as an integrated whole. The advantage of articulating alternative standards is that in most cases irreversible cessation of circulatory and respiratory function is a sufficient basis for diagnosing death. The need to evaluate brain functions arises only when the patient is supported on a respirator.

3. Brain death as an extended means of determining death beyond the heart-lung criteria.

This is evident in the Michigan statute:

> A person will be considered dead if in the announced opinion of a physician, based on ordinary standards of medical practice in the community, there is the irreversible cessation of spontaneous respiratory and circulatory function. If artificial means of support preclude a determination that these functions have ceased, a person will be considered dead if in the

announced opinion of a physician, based on ordinary standards of medical practice in the community, there is the irreversible cessation of spontaneous brain function. Death will
have occurred at the time when the relevant functions
ceased.[24]

This statute is also limited by the ambiguity of "spontaneous
brain function." It has the advantage of recognizing that traditional criteria of heart and lung functioning can be used in most
cases, but not in the exceptional case when artificial life-support
mechanisms are being used.

**4. Brain death as a substitute determination of death over
heart-lung determination.**

This is found in the Georgia statute:

A person may be pronounced dead if it is determined that the
person has suffered an irreversible cessation of brain function.
There shall be independent confirmation of the death by
another physician.[25]

This statute is subject to all the ambiguities of the meaning of
"brain function" when it is left unqualified. It implicitly recognizes the traditional heart-lung criteria since the cessation of the
heart and lungs represents specific criteria by which the irreversible cessation of brain functions is determined.

While not every state has yet adopted a brain-oriented statute, no state completely rejects the concept of brain death.
Although variations in the determination-of-death statutes surveyed above are obvious, three common features prevail. First,
the brain-oriented statutes are saying that when the entire brain
has irreversibly ceased to function, then the person is dead in
spite of the fact that the heartbeat may go on with mechanical
help. Second, none of them depend on the concept of cerebral
death. This suggests that while the irreversible loss of consciousness and social interaction may be grounds for allowing the individual (or proxy) to refuse life-prolonging treatment, it is not recognized as legal grounds for declaring the patient "dead." None

of the existing or proposed legislation is endorsing any difficult-to-determine quality of life standards that would flow from the concept of cerebral death. Third, the statutes are careful not to give legislative force to any particular set of medical diagnostic criteria for determining death. Since the techniques of diagnosis are continually evolving, the statutes address only very general physiological standards for determining death. The law simply requires that these physiological standards be tested by the accepted standards of medical practice.

The model statute proposed by the President's Commission (model 2 above), often designated as the Uniform Determination of Death Act, has become the major focus in the debate over brain-death legislation. The United States Bishop's Committee for Pro-Life Activities opposes it as well as determination-of-death statutes in general.[26] Fr. Ed Bryce, chairman of the committee, objects on three grounds:[27]

1. There is no demonstrated need for such laws.

Legislation is not the way to remedy the confusion that exists on the determination of death; education is. Furthermore, no state law forbids using brain-oriented criteria for determining death anyway.

2. The proposed law is not likely to achieve uniformity among the states.

Each state is capable of amending the proposed uniform code. Moreover, since the statute would legalize criteria which have not yet been understood or accepted by the general public, it may open new avenues of litigation as physicians follow it without fully informing patients' families.

3. Such legislation can become the stepping stone to authorizing active killing of the dying but not yet dead.

The statute is designed to assure that dead patients are not treated as living. It does not guarantee that the living will not be treated as dead.

The Pennsylvania Catholic Conference supports determination-of-death legislation and the proposed statute of the President's Commission because of its potential for preventing legal recognition of less restrictive standards, such as quality-of-life standards that would flow from statutes based only on cerebral death. The conference answers some objections to determination-of-death legislation like those made by the Bishops' Pro-Life Committee. Against the claim that such legislation is not necessary, the conference sees the real issue to be not one of necessity but of helpfulness. With the medical world now complicated by technology, determination-of-death statutes would be helpful to all concerned, especially the one whose death is being determined. And against the claim that such legislation will lead to authorizing active killing of the dying, the conference sees that such an occurrence will come about only with a change of attitudes and amendments that are radical departures from the proposed and already existing laws. It will not be the result of the present law.[28]

The Catholic Health Association has no legal or moral objection to the determination-of-death statute proposed by the President's Commission, but it finds the education of physicians and the general public on medical and philosophical aspects of brain death to be a higher priority.

> The mere presence of a law on the books may not sway the brain dead patient's spouse who sees a conflict between religion and removal of the support of the respirator. The mere presence of a law on the books may not prevent a physician who fears liability from petitioning a court for permission to disconnect the respirator. The mere presence of a law on the books may not prevent a criminal defendant, desperate to be acquitted of murder, from accusing medical personnel of having actually caused the decedent's death. And the mere presence of a law on the books may not prevent the next of kin, by reason of greed or vindictiveness, from suing the doctor for malpractice and wrongful death.

> The UDDA and the other brain death statutes are not a cure-all. They are not the end of the issue. In fact, they represent

only the beginning of the educational process needed to avoid the scenarios mentioned above.[29]

This survey of the legal discussion shows a growing consensus today of the acceptance of brain-related criteria for determining death. The entire discussion on the determination of death shows us that the concept of death must be kept distinct from the criteria for determining death. Our concept of death is what moves us closer to the hard moral choices of judging the kind of relationship we need to have with the individual and the kind of care that remains appropriate. Some of the moral issues surrounding these hard choices will be the topic of the next chapter.

2
The Moral Issues

Before we consider the spectrum of positions on euthanasia, we need to consider some of the more significant issues at stake in taking those positions. Where one stands on these issues has a great deal to do with where one stands on euthanasia. At least four issues stand out: (1) the principle of the sanctity of life; (2) the extent of dominion over life and death; (3) the difference between killing and allowing to die (or acts of commission and omission); (4) the meaning of the distinction between ordinary and extraordinary means of treatment to sustain life.

Sanctity of Life

Daniel Callahan asks, "If, then, some minimal degree of moral consensus is necessary on matters of life and death, what is it and on what can it be based?"[1] His answer: the sanctity of life. Callahan goes on to say, "On the basis of this principle, moral rules have been framed, human rights claimed and defended, and cultural, political, and social priorities established."[2] Sometimes "sanctity of life" is expressed as "respect or reverence for life," "the dignity of human life," "the value of human life," or even "the right to life." Yet "sanctity of life" seems to be the most common expression. But what are the sources of this principle? What does it mean and how does it function as a foundational principle? After we have explored answers to these questions in this chapter, we will be ready to address another: How can "sanctity of life" be used in moral decisions and in the formation of a moral consensus on euthanasia? The various answers to this question will be evident in the spectrum of positions surveyed in the next chapter.

Sources of the Sanctity of Life Principle

"Sanctity of life" has both religious and non-religious sources. Religiously, Catholics and Protestants have pushed the sanctity of life principle back to its divine origins and have invested it with religious meaning based on a variety of Christian doctrines, such as creation and redemption, the immortality of the soul and a religious understanding of the human person, to name a few. James Gustafson regards the attitude of respect for life to be "evoked, grounded, and informed" by the religious belief that God is Creator and Sustainer of life and wills its well-being.[3] Norman St. John-Stevas, who has written extensively on the sanctity of life from a Roman Catholic perspective, situates the principle within a religious understanding of the human person:

> The value of human life for the Christian in the first century A.D., as today, rested not on its development of a superior sentience but on the unique character of the union of body and soul, both destined for eternal life. The right to life thus has a theological foundation.... Respect for the lives of *others* because of their eternal destiny is the essence of the Christian teaching.[4]

Also from a religious view, Paul Ramsey makes the point that sanctity of life is not a function of the worth any human person attributes to life, but that its primary value lies in the relation of life to God:

> One grasps the religious outlook upon the sanctity of human life only if he sees that this life is asserted to be *surrounded* by sanctity that need not be in a man; that the most dignity a man ever possesses is a dignity that is alien to him.... A man's dignity is an overflow from God's dealing with him, and not

primarily an anticipation of anything he will ever be by himself alone.[5]

These religious viewpoints seem to affirm that the sanctity of life,
or human dignity and value, is not intrinsic to human life as
such, nor is it dependent on the evaluation of other human
beings or on human achievement. Rather, the sanctity of human
life, or human worth, as an "alien dignity" is ultimately conferred
by God. But only those who accept the full theological framework
for this conviction are able to affirm that life is always a guaran-
teed value or dignity because the only way life truly exists is in
"covenant," or in relationship to God.

This grounding of the sanctity of life in religious convictions
may serve the believer well, but what about the non-believer? Are
there any non-religious groundings of this principle? There are.
Two can serve to represent them.

The first is from the general moral theory of Daniel C.
Maguire. According to Maguire, the principle of the sanctity of
life expresses the foundational moral experience of the precious-
ness of persons.[6] The experience of the value of persons answers
the question, "Why be moral at all?" Without this sort of experience, morality becomes a matter of self-interest. Maguire
describes the importance of this foundational moral experience
this way:

> The foundation of morality is *the experience of the value of*
> *persons and their environment.* This experience is *the* distinc-
> tively human and humanizing experience and the gateway to
> personhood. It is this experience that sets us apart from beast
> and barbarian. It is the seed of civilization, the root of culture,
> and the badge of distinctively human consciousness. Without
> an in-depth participation in this experience, morality would
> seem a meaningless intrusion on our whim and fancy, and
> moral language would be non-sense. If human activities, insti-
> tutions, and religions do not enhance this experience, they are
> negligible and indeed objectionable, for they are failing at the
> constitutional level of human existence.[7]

Another non-religious grounding for the sanctity of life
comes from sociologist Edward Shils. He asks, "Is human life

really sacred?" and responds, "I answer that it is, self-evidently. Its sacredness is the most primordial of experiences."[8] He suggests that one of the factors which contributes to raising the question about the sanctity of life in the first place is the diminishing force of Christian beliefs to provide criteria for judgment about the worth of human life. As he says, "The cognitive content of Christian doctrine, and above all the grandiose Christian symbolization of man's origin and destiny, have now lost much of their appeal."[9]

Shils contends that if a moral consensus on the sanctity of life is to be formed, it cannot depend on religious beliefs but will have to be founded on common human experience. But is there such an experience which yields the conviction about the sanctity of life? Shils thinks so. He finds it in the primordial experience of being alive, in the fear of extinction, in the spontaneous revulsion to contrived interventions and unnatural destruction of human life, and in the sense of awe one feels before one's own vitality and that of the species. He calls this experience the "protoreligious or natural metaphysic" of the sanctity of life. He describes it this way:

> The chief feature of the protoreligious, "natural metaphysic" is the affirmation that life *is* sacred. It is believed to be sacred not because it is a manifestation of a transcendent creator from whom life comes ... [rather] the idea of sacredness is generated by the primordial experience of being alive, of experiencing the elemental sensation of vitality and the elemental fear of its extinction.[10]

Shils does not regard this primordial experience of vitality to be a subconscious holdover from past Christian beliefs, but, in fact, he maintains that Christian doctrines have been sustained and made effective because of this primordial experience. This secular humanist position seems to be saying that sanctity is intrinsic to human life and is disclosed through the primordial experience of life. Sanctity of life requires no justification outside human life, and it finds its ultimate validity in human experience.

Meaning and Function of the Sanctity of Life Principle

While trying to establish the validity of first principles is always difficult, and objections can be raised to this attempt,[11] what matters in the euthanasia discussion is the widespread acceptance of the sanctity of life as a general principle. The Christian approach and the experiential approach of a natural metaphysic may differ on the source of the sanctity of life, but they agree on its value as a first principle. The reason for the agreement may ultimately be pragmatic. For instance, Shils writes, "Without a widespread affirmation of the sanctity of life . . . as the basic guiding principle of social life, we will be hopelessly adrift."[12] This is based on his credo, "If life were not viewed and experienced as sacred, then nothing else would be sacred."[13] St. John-Stevas puts it this way, "Once exceptions are made [to the principle of the sanctity of life], the whole structure of human rights is undermined."[14] Both seem to be saying that if we want any values honored, then we need to postulate the principle of the sanctity of life. Likewise, James Gustafson: "[Life] is received as the necessary condition for any value, any well-being, and thus is received as a value, as a good, and thus deserves respect."[15]

In light of these arguments, sanctity of life seems to be an acceptable basis for approaching moral consensus on matters of life and death. Yet it remains an ambiguous principle, open to a variety of moral rules, duties and positions. James Gustafson, for example, realizes that defending respect for life without requiring that human physical life be invincible places moral choices on a slippery slope. Respect for life in itself is not sufficient to determine what a proper course of action ought to be to ensure what constitutes "respect" or whose life ought to be protected.[16] David C. Thomasma illustrates this very well in his *An Apology for the Value of Human Life.*[17] His work shows that a commitment to the sanctity of life or the "irreducible value inherent in human beings," as he expresses it, does not confine us to one particular moral, political, or religious position. Considerable latitude still exists. "Consequently," he concludes, "considerable discussion and debate would still be necessary before our society reached a consensus about macro and micro human life issues."[18] The next chapter will survey the wide spectrum of positions that are being taken in this discussion based on the sanctity of life principle. There we will see that the widespread affirmation of this principle does not lead to any unified consensus on what it implies.

Why, then, hold on to this principle if it is so vague? How does it function in the euthanasia discussion? Daniel Callahan answers this way:

> It expresses a willingness to treat human life with consideration, to give it dignity, to commit ourselves to its furtherance. The function of specific rules is to implement and give concreteness to these commitments; in turn these commitments, as summed up in the principle, will serve to judge the adequacy of the rules.[19]

In other words, this principle functions the way abstract, formal principles generally function in ethics. It does not itself tell us what to do, but acts as a standard for assessing the concrete material norms which do try to tell us what to do. More specifically, as a formal principle, "sanctity of life" points us in the direction of enhancing the well-being of human life, inclines us to form certain kinds of rules to protect human life, engenders an attitude which fosters a strong bias in favor of human life, and encourages us to act in ways consistent with this bias. For example, in the euthanasia discussion, one of the material norms implied by the sanctity of life principle is that no one has the right unjustly to deprive another of bodily life. The sanctity of life principle forces us to ask whether following this norm will truly enhance a person's life or not. But the principle of the sanctity of life does not entail by way of logical deduction any set ordering of moral rules. It only points us in a life-affirming and life-protecting direction.[20] So, whether given a religious grounding or not, the sanctity of life principle remains best protected through human efforts to form and implement rules designed to protect and foster life. The diversity of positions surveyed in the next chapter will show how much this fundamental principle has all the imprints of human handling.

Dominion and Stewardship

Closely related to the sanctity of life principle, and often treated in conjunction with it, are the theological principles of God's dominion and human stewardship. Theological beliefs about God's sovereignty and human stewardship are invoked particularly by those espousing a Christian religious perspective on the sanctity and inviolability of human life. One sometimes hears the charge that anyone who intervenes to hasten death, or anyone who foregoes treatment in order to let the patient die, is "playing God." The charge aims to underscore that since God is the Author of life and death, the time for life's ending belongs to God and not to us. One's understanding of dominion and stewardship is at stake here. In this section, as in the one on the sanctity of life, we will be concerned with the source, meaning and function of these theological principles in the euthanasia discussion.

Source of the Principles of Dominion and Stewardship

Central to both Catholic and Protestant theology is the conviction that God is Lord of life and death. This conviction is another way of affirming that the ultimate value and sanctity of human life comes from God. To confess that God is the Lord of life and death affirms the fundamental distinction between Creator and created, and it affirms that as creatures, humans owe their existence, value and ultimate destiny to God. These affirmations imply that no one can ever claim total mastery over one's own or another's life.

The source of these convictions lies in the same religious doctrines which give us the principle of the sanctity of life. For instance, from his religious doctrine of the human person, Norman St. John-Stevas is able to claim, "Man is not absolutely master of his own life and body. He has no *dominium* over it, but holds it in trust for God's purposes."[21] Similarly, Bernard Häring argues from his fundamental conviction that human life is a sacred gift of God and affirms, "Life is entrusted to man's freedom and co-responsibility. He is not an independent lord of his life but a steward under the sovereignty of God."[22] Paul Ramsey, with his theme of "alien dignity" for human life, reverberates within the Protestant tradition with echoes of Karl Barth's theology of creation. Ramsey emphasizes life as God's loan to us. He argues that we must respect our own lives and the lives of others not only because life is grounded in God, but also because God has given us life as a value to be held in trust and to be used according to God's will. We ought to imitate God who has said "Yes" to life.[23]

Meaning and Function of Dominion and Stewardship

Dominion and stewardship have found their way into the euthanasia discussion through the many moralists who have followed the third argument of St. Thomas against suicide. There Thomas argues that, as Creator, God alone is Lord over life and death.

> To kill oneself is never allowed because life is a gift to man from God who alone has authority to kill and to give life. Hence whoever takes his own life sins against God in the same way that he who kills another's slave sins against the slave's master, and as he sins who takes on himself for judgment a matter not entrusted to him (II-II, q. 64, a. 5).

Also in this article, St. Thomas affirms that determining the end of human life is not something subject to a person's free judgment:

> That a person has dominion over himself is because he is endowed with free choice. Thanks to that free choice a man is at liberty to dispose of himself with respect to those things in this life which are subject to his freedom. But the passage from this life to a happier one is not one of those things, for one's passage from this life is subject to the will and power of God (II-II, q. 65, a. 5, ad 3).

In this argument, human persons have only a right to the use of human life, not to dominion over human life. What makes killing forbidden is that it usurps a divine prerogative and violates divine rights.

The Roman Catholic moral tradition has regarded taking innocent human life as "intrinsically evil" by defect of right *(ex defectu juris in agente)* because no human person has the right to assume such dominion over life. Thomas J. O'Donnell expresses the Catholic tradition's use of this argument in his distinction between "absolute" and "useful" dominion. Absolute dominion is power over one's final end; useful dominion is power restricted by the higher rights of others.[24] In his most recently revised medical-moral textbook, *Medicine and Christian Morality*,[25] he speaks of "prerogative" instead of "dominion" but comes to the same conclusion—namely, when dealing with human life we have only the right to use and the responsibility of stewardship. The absolute dominion or prerogative is an exclusively divine prerogative.[26]

David F. Kelly has shown in his comprehensive work, *The Emergence of Roman Catholic Medical Ethics in North America*,[27] that prior to Vatican II (1962–1965) the application of the theological principle of God's sovereignty (together with the principle of the redemptive value of suffering) functioned primarily as a source of motivation to support medical-moral conclusions drawn from natural law physicalism or ecclesiastical positivism. Kelly finds that the principles of God's sovereignty and the redemptive value of suffering expressed two aspects of the one theological concern of the human person's relationship to God as Creator. Since Vatican II, however, the use of the principle of God's sovereignty has respected the paradox, mystery and myth inherent in it. This principle no longer functions in a way logically dependent on decisions reached on other grounds. Rather, it functions as a hermeneutical theme to interpret the more general question of the meaning of human life.[28]

James Gustafson, in his Marquette lecture *The Contributions of Theology to Medical Ethics,* has explored the hermeneutical function of theological beliefs in medical ethics and shows that theological beliefs provide a fundamental moral perspective on medical care by "informing certain attitudes" toward human life, and by "informing a basic ethical intentionality that gives direction to intervention in the biological processes of life."[29] These theological contributions, however, are not sufficient to determine precise solutions to individual problems in health care. Gustafson insists that additional ethical reflection is required to determine precisely what is valued about human life, and what principles, rights and obligations are to give moral direction to interventions in human life.[30]

The precise way in which the theological principle of God's sovereignty as a hermeneutical theme ought to be applied to issues pertaining to interventions in human life remains undetermined. Moralists vary in the way they use this theme in trying to balance the creature and co-creator tensions in issues of medical ethics. For example, Bernard Häring makes an explicitly theological argument against any direct intervention in the dying process to end life. He argues that the freedom of the creature does not extend to the free choice of forcing death to take us at the time and under the conditions we stipulate. For Häring, we exercise the fullness of our freedom in death by our free acceptance of death. Only this exercise of freedom which admits to powerlessness in the face of death is the truthful admission of our existence as creatures of God.[31]

Richard Westley, on the other hand, challenges such an argument. He equates Creator and the creature more univocally than Häring does. On the basis of an incarnational faith, Westley claims that the divine and human are so wedded to one another as to eliminate any talk of divine and human prerogatives. For Westley, the mystery of the incarnation tells us that God has chosen to make divine work our own. Since God lives in us, whatever belongs to divine dominion also belongs to us.[32] Westley also challenges absolute sovereignty and limited stewardship by exploring the meaning of life as a "gift" from God. As Westley sees it, if life is given as a gift, then it is subject to our freedom and to speak of stewardship is out of place in this context.[33]

Like Westley, Daniel C. Maguire makes an equation of Creator and creature but on different grounds. Maguire draws upon an interpretation of the human person as being an "image of God," a co-creator with God and participator in God's providence. On this basis, he finds an opening for a more expansive moral authority over life and death than Häring and the traditional interpretations of dominion and stewardship would allow.[34]

Bruno Schüller would challenge any position which argues against euthanasia solely on the basis of dominion. For Schüller, the principle of dominion simply restates what needs to be proved:

> Indeed "not to be able to kill oneself" and "not to have dominion over the substance of one's life" are synonymous phrases. If we may say God *alone* is Lord over the life and death of a man, this is in the context merely an expression of that which is to be proved.[35]

These examples demonstrate a few ways in which the theological principle of God's dominion functions in contemporary medical ethics. Westley and Maguire do not respect the fundamental distinction between Creator and creature the way Häring or the longer Catholic theological tradition does. Schüller shows the limits of dominion as a theological principle in this moral argument. It presupposes what is to be proven. The positions surveyed in the next chapter will show even more thoroughly that no clear unilateral manner of applying this theological principle as a hermeneutical theme exists in reflections on euthanasia today. The next chapter will also show that "sanctity of life" and "limited dominion" must combine with a variety of other ethical considerations in order to determine a position on euthanasia.

Killing and Letting Die

The distinction between killing and letting die, or between acts of commission and omission, is at the heart of the euthanasia discussion. For instance, if we prohibit the intentional termination of innocent human life, no matter what its stage of development or quality, then on what basis are we permitted to stop treatment by turning off the respirator of a permanently comatose, but alive, patient? The distinction between commission and omission is at stake here. This is the issue that gives rise to qualifying euthanasia as active or passive, positive or negative.

The stance one takes on this issue greatly affects the stance one takes on euthanasia. For some, the distinction simply designates a descriptive difference in actions to terminate life. So, once we decide not to prolong one's dying, whether we actively intervene to cause death or passively allow the person to die makes no moral difference. Others will hold that the distinction does have moral significance, but that this significance dissolves when the patient is irretrievably dying or is beyond the reach of human care. Another alternative is that the distinction always has "moral bite" so that one ought always to refrain from intervening to hasten death, but one may withhold or withdraw therapies that will simply prolong the person's dying. These alternatives and their various degrees of expression will be evident in the next chapter. For now we are primarily interested in the sorts of arguments that have been advanced to promote or challenge the claims to a moral difference between commission and omission.

Moral Equivalence of Killing and Letting Die

James Rachels represents one way of challenging the claim to the moral difference between killing and letting die. His argument has received a significant amount of attention since it was published in the nation's most prestigious medical journal, *The New England Journal of Medicine*.[36] One of his arguments challenges the preference for letting a person die on the basis of the unnecessary suffering which would be caused by prolonging life. Rachels also challenges the argument that says in allowing the patient to die no one really does anything and the patient dies of "natural" causes. Rachels argues that even in letting someone die, the doctor really does do something. The doctor lets the patient die. This, too, should be included, along with not administering therapy, in the total description of what is happening in attending to the dying. He reinforces this position by attacking the fear of being the "cause" of someone's death. He says that we think it is bad to cause someone's death because we think death is an evil. But once we have decided that death is no greater evil for a patient than the patient's continued existence, then causing death would be a good thing.

Rachels also challenges the argument that killing is always worse than letting someone die by comparing two cases which are exactly alike except for this one difference. In one case, Smith stands to gain a large inheritance from the death of his six-year-old cousin. Smith wants the child dead, so he drowns him in the bathtub. In the second case, Jones stands to gain from the death of his six-year-old cousin. He wants the child dead. As he enters the bathroom, he is delighted to see the child slip, hit his head, and fall face down in the water. Jones allows the child to die. The only difference in these cases is that Smith killed the child, while Jones merely let him die. The intentions are the same, and so are the consequences. Rachels concludes from these cases that killing and letting die are the same from the moral point of view. What makes killing seem worse are the motives for personal gain, and the fact that healthy persons lost their lives.

Related to these cases is the argument from the priority given to the duty not to harm over the duty to help. This would seem to indicate a morally significant difference between killing and letting die since killing violates the duty not to harm, whereas letting die is merely a failure to give help. However, Rachels holds that these differences of duty vanish in cases in which it would be easy for us to help someone close at hand and in which no great personal sacrifice is required. Such is the situation in the doctor-patient relationship in instances of euthanasia. Therefore, the presumed moral difference between killing and letting die does not hold.

Moral Difference Between Killing and Letting Die

The arguments put forth by Rachels, especially in the example of the two cases, do show that some omissions are morally as wrong as actively killing. Even those who hold to a moral difference in the distinction would say this. For instance, Grisez and Boyle agree with Rachels that omission counts as an immoral act of killing when it is the way to realize one's intention that a person die.[37] This is in line with the mainstream of the Roman Catholic tradition and is reflected in the definition of "euthanasia" in the Vatican *Declaration on Euthanasia,* promulgated by the Vatican Congregation for the Doctrine of the Faith, June 26, 1980:

> By euthanasia is understood an action or omission which of itself or by intention causes death, in order that in this way all suffering may be eliminated.

The phrase "which of itself or by intention causes death" is necessary in order to affirm that not taking steps to prolong life when such steps are required is just as much the cause of death as a lethal injection would be. Likewise, refusing treatment with the intention to end one's life is suicide.

Where Rachels differs from the Catholic position, and what Rachels fails to show, is that not all omissions are wrongful acts of killing. "Intention" makes the difference. The Catholic tradition of maintaining a moral difference between killing and letting die on the basis of intentional discriminations is a complex one. Only a brief review is possible here.

The Catholic tradition has long defended the principle of double effect, the code name for the distinction between the direct and indirect intention in areas of human life.[38] This principle defines the conditions which must be met if an action resulting in both good and bad effects is to be morally permissible. The four conditions are: (1) the action in itself, apart from its effects, is not morally evil; (2) the evil effect is not produced by means of the good effect; (3) the evil effect is not intended; (4) a proportionate reason supports the action in spite of the evil consequences. For example, in caring for the terminally ill, physicians sometimes find themselves facing the conflict of not wanting to kill their patients but wanting to relieve their pain. However, in some instances relieving pain indirectly kills the patient. This death becomes the indirect effect of an action intended to relieve pain, the direct effect. Such a death would be morally permissible according to the principle of double effect since this death lies outside the intention of the act and is supported by a proportionate reason. This is affirmed by the Ethical and Religious Directives of Catholic Health Facilities:

> It is not euthanasia to give a dying person sedatives and anal-
> gesics for the alleviation of pain, when such a measure is
> judged necessary, even though they may deprive the patient of
> the use of reason, or shorten his life (#29).

The Directives also say, "The directly intended termination of any patient's life, even at his own request, is always morally wrong" (#10).

The insight behind this principle with its distinction of direct and indirect intention is that the moral quality of an act is affected by the intention, or attitude, of the will toward the evil done. But in time, the terms "direct" and "indirect" became attached to certain physical actions alone. Thus we have norms formulated in these terms, such as "no direct killing" and "no direct sterilization."[39] Formulations like these show that the procedures were now defining the intention, rather than the intention defining the moral quality of the procedure. Consequently, directness and indirectness became all-important in determining morality to the exclusion of determining whether or not there was a proportionate reason for causing the evil effect.

The past two decades, however, have witnessed a vigorous re-evaluation not only of the conditions which make up the principle of double effect but also of the moral relevance of the principle itself. I have reviewed this shift in my other book in this series, *What Are They Saying About Moral Norms?*[40] According to the present state of this discussion among some revisionist moral theologians, "direct" and "indirect" are no longer tied to the physical actions in themselves nor to the intentions themselves. In short, according to the opinion of some theologians today, the moral significance of an action no longer depends on directness or indirectness itself. Rather, the distinction between direct and indirect intention serves to identify a descriptive difference between actions involving non-moral evils (such as pain, suffering, death) by showing what is being sought, by what means, and in what circumstances. But direct or indirect intention alone does not designate the total moral significance of an act. "Due proportion," or the proper relationship of all aspects of the action taken as a whole (what is being sought, by what means, in what circumstances), reveals the moral significance of an action.[41]

The President's Commission rejects the distinction of intended and unintended but foreseeable consequences as grounds for assigning moral significance to actions and omissions. One reason is the great unclarity in trying to determine whether a particular aspect of an action is intended because it is intricately part of the "means" by which the end is achieved, or whether it is merely an unintended but foreseeable consequence. For example, the choice not to have a potentially life-saving operation can be done with the intention to hasten death or to avoid additional suffering while dying (with death being the unintended but "foreseeable consequence"). Also, the commission rejects the distinction as a way to excuse anyone from the responsibility of considering all the consequences of one's choices. A person is responsible for all reasonably foreseeable results of an action and not just those directly intended. For the commission the real moral issue entailed in this distinction is not that death is forbidden as a means to relieve suffering, but that it is made acceptable as a foreseeable consequence. The real issue, as the commission sees it, is

> whether or not the decisionmakers have considered the full range of foreseeable effects, have knowingly accepted whatever risk of death is entailed, and have found the risk to be justified in light of the paucity and undesirability of other opinions.[42]

All the discussion on "intention" in recent years shows us that "intention" does not adequately establish the moral significance between commission and omission. Robert Veatch has recognized this and so amalgamates intention with four other reasons which, when taken together, contribute to supporting a moral difference between killing and letting die.[43] In addition to the argument based on intention, Veatch also cites the argument that commissions and omissions are psychologically different— that is, we feel differently about active killing than we do about withdrawing treatments. This argument, however, entails all the difficulty of trying to determine the origin of these feelings, whether consistent patterns of difference in those feelings exist, and whether these differences can be attributed to an accurate moral perception. Since the link between the psychological impact of a decision and its moral rightness or wrongness is difficult to establish, he concludes that the psychological difference is not conclusive evidence to sustain a moral difference in the distinction.[44]

Veatch also cites the argument that active killing would conflict with the role of the physician to preserve life. Yet the counter-argument says that if active killing were to be practiced at all, the physician would be the one in the best position to use the most humane technique. But grounding the moral difference of the commission-omission distinction on the role of the physician presupposes that the physician should be the one doing the killing, that society regards the physician as a preserver of life, that killing would conflict with that more than allowing to die would, and that we would not be able to restrict physicians in any effective way to killing only in special cases. Veatch judges these to be quite tenuous and so seeks other grounds upon which to consider the distinction morally different.[45]

Another argument can be made on the basis of consequences. This argument says that if we accept active killing for mercy we are opening the way for other active killings. This gives rise to two forms of the wedge argument. One is logical and the other empirical. The logical form follows from making an exception to the prohibition of killing. The empirical form follows when active killing for mercy leads to active killing for other reasons and the people involved are not able to make relevant moral distinctions in the different kinds of cases. Veatch sees in this wedge argument a potential moral difference between omission and commission.[46]

His final argument is that the cause of death is different in commissions and omissions. From the standpoint of moral responsibility and culpability, acts of commission and omission seem to be different. In some cases where the relationship between parties includes the specific moral duty to provide life-prolonging treatment, some omissions are morally as wrong as actively killing. This is the case in the two examples which Rachels uses. But not all omissions are as wrong as actively killing. Veatch holds that the omission of a treatment by a physician, when the physician is instructed to omit it, is not the same as acting to cause the death of a patient. The "cause" of death would be different in these instances. The difference in the cause of death, then, does not adequately account for the moral difference between commissions and omissions.[47]

Like Veatch, Daniel C. Maguire[48] and Paul T. Menzel[49] explore a variety of ways in which omission and commission can make a real moral difference. They seem to agree that while there may be many good reasons to hold the distinction as morally relevant, no one of these reasons is totally convincing by itself. Veatch summarizes these findings well when he says:

> In the end the case for a moral difference between actively killing the dying patient and withdrawing treatment in order that the patient may die will have to rest upon all of these arguments taken together, not on any one of them alone. The individual differences may be subtle, some more persuasive than others. Combined, however, their impact is somewhat more impressive. Of course, combining several unpersuasive arguments cannot make a persuasive one, but several possible arguments taken together can increase the possibility of the conclusion.[50]

Other arguments in favor of the distinction invoke certain theological convictions to support it. For example, Gilbert Meilaender tries to make explicit the religious underpinnings of Ramsey's position of maintaining a moral significance in the distinction by situating it in the context of the Christian story of God's action with us in creation and redemption. The force of the distinction comes in our understanding of death in the context of this story. On the one hand, death is something to be resisted, since the creation story shows it to be the result of turning from God and toward sin. On the other hand, death is something to be acknowledged, since the story of redemption shows it to be the means through which God is victorious in Christ. This way of understanding death gives "moral bite" to the distinction by setting limits on care. It does not support expressions of care

which include forcing a person to the end of life, nor does it support holding on desperately to life when the end finally comes. In
the Christian context, actions of either sort do not reflect the
shape of God's actions toward human well-being.[51]

Others argue in favor of the distinction on moral and practical grounds. For example, Tom L. Beauchamp combines a rule-
utilitarian and wedge argument to defend the distinction. His
rule-utilitarian position seeks a rule which, if adopted by society,
would lead to better consequences for the common good than
any other competing rule would. The rule prohibiting killing but
allowing the dying patient to die leads to better consequences
than a rule permitting restricted killing. His wedge argument
leads him to conclude that rules permitting killing could too easily lead to reducing respect for human life. Beauchamp
concludes:

> And if, as I believe, moral principles against active killing have
> the deep and continuously civilizing effect of promoting
> respect for life, and if principles which allow passively letting
> die ... do not themselves cut against this effect, then this
> seems an important reason for the maintenance of the active/
> passive distinction.[52]

James Childress favors the distinction on the basis of a very
practical consideration. He finds the distinction to be inextrica-
bly tied up with our understanding of medical care. To dissolve
the distinction and allow physicians to kill dying patients "would
so alter the moral ethos of medicine as to necessitate a new basis
of trust."[53] Trust in the context of health care is the expectation
that everyone will respect moral limits and work together for our
health and life and do us no harm.

As this brief survey shows, the distinction between killing
and allowing to die is subtle and complex. The preponderance of
evidence favors a moral difference for the distinction, though
ways for arguing to this difference vary. Maintaining a moral difference between killing and allowing to die has been common-
place in the Catholic medical-moral tradition. It lies behind the
prudential application of another important distinction which

has been receiving a great deal of attention—the distinction between ordinary and extraordinary means of treatment.

Ordinary and Extraordinary Means

The significance of the commission-omission distinction becomes even more apparent as it intersects with the principle of ordinary and extraordinary means of treatment. According to this principle, the failure to use ordinary means of preserving life is an act of euthanasia. It is the moral equivalent of direct killing. However, not to use extraordinary means to preserve life is permissible. Allowing the patient to die by omitting extraordinary means is morally different from direct killing. Such is the moral significance of the ordinary/extraordinary distinction, which has come under critical review in recent years. In this section we are concerned primarily with what this distinction means and some of the alternatives being suggested for it.

Standard Moral Meaning of Ordinary and Extraordinary Means

The distinction of ordinary and extraordinary means is staple fare in the Catholic medical-moral tradition. Often one hears in popular circles that refusing extraordinary means is "Catholic euthanasia." But, when properly understood, the distinction enshrines the wisdom which tells us that enough is enough.

In the beginning, the Roman Catholic moralists who worked out the distinction did not have in mind those who had already begun to die and for whom treatment would be entirely useless. They had in mind, rather, those whose lives could be prolonged by radical measures, like surgery. The distinction dates back to the sixteenth century where it emerged to address the issues of the pain suffered in surgical operations which were practically unbearable because of the lack of anaesthesia, and because their outcome was uncertain due to the lack of antiseptics to fight infection. In 1595 Bañez introduced the terms "ordinary" and "extraordinary" to designate those means of preserving life which bring negligible pain and those which cause agonizing, unbearable pain.[54] The terms have remained in use while developments in the science and art of medicine have changed the circumstances calling for their application. Gerald Kelly, the leading Catholic expert on medical-moral matters prior to Vatican II and the period of modern medical ethics, reflects the historical development of these terms as well as what has become of the standard rendering of this distinction in the Catholic tradition in his now classic interpretation:

> *Ordinary* means of preserving life are all medicines, treatments, and operations, which offer a reasonable hope of benefit for the patient and which can be obtained and used without excessive expense, pain, or other inconvenience.

> *Extraordinary* means of preserving life . . . [are] all medicines, treatments, and operations, which cannot be obtained or used without excessive expense, pain, or other inconvenience, or which, if used, would not offer a reasonable hope of benefit.[55]

Pius XII reflects this meaning of these terms in his famous address "The Prolongation of Life" given in 1957.[56]

Kelly's rendering shows that these terms are not merely descriptive but evaluative. They do not simply describe the ease or difficulty in using a particular means of treatment, but they make a judgment regarding the obligation of their use. Ordinary means are morally imperative; extraordinary means are morally permissible, not obligatory. *Burden* (or convenience) and *benefit* (or usefulness) are the two conditions which must be determined in order to make a proper moral use of these terms.[57] But in specific cases, determining the degree of burden and benefit of a given procedure is not easy. These conditions admit of many variations. The Vatican *Declaration on Euthanasia* recognizes this when it suggests what a correct judgment of means ought to consider:

> It will be possible to make a correct judgment as to the means by studying the type of treatment to be used, its degree of complexity or risk, its cost and the possibilities of using it, and comparing these elements with the result that can be expected,

taking into account the state of the sick person and his or her physical and moral resources.

As the Declaration shows, the degree of burden and benefit is relative to the total condition of the patient. This cannot be determined by a computer but must be determined according to the reasonable judgment of prudent and conscientious persons. The judgment of a patient with the mental capacity to understand the medical situation and make a decision about it ought to be given preference. In the case of a patient who does not have this capacity, the judgment of the patient's proxy ought to be given preference.

Contrasting the Medical and Moral Meanings of the Distinction

Part of the difficulty and confusion with the moral use and meaning of these terms comes from their being associated with a medical use and meaning. Paul Ramsey cites three differences in the way doctors and moralists use these terms.[58] First, ordinary and extraordinary means in medicine are relative to the present "state of the art" of medical practice, not the state of the person. Ordinary means, then, are the routine, usual or customary therapies in medical practice relative to a certain ailment or disease. Extraordinary means, in the medical sense, are whatever would be novel or experimental. With this understanding we could make a list of medically ordinary (standard) procedures and medically extraordinary ones (experimental) at any particular time in the development of medicine. For example, in 1930 a blood transfusion was medically extraordinary. In 1960 hemodialysis was. Today both are quite ordinary.

However, we could not make any such list of treatments from a moral point of view. Morally, ordinary and extraordinary means are relative to the patient's total condition. This means that non-medical factors must also be considered, like the person's value history—which includes beliefs, fears, hopes, life style, personal and social responsibilities, ways of valuing life, and the like—as well as the patient's emotional and spiritual capacity, degree of affective interaction, and economic situation.

While the medical and moral meanings of these terms may over-
lap in some instances, they are not co-extensive.

Secondly, Ramsey cites a difference between doctors and
moralists in the decision to stop extraordinary treatment. For the
doctor, the decision to stop life-sustaining treatment is much
more difficult than the decision not to start it. But for the moralist, the decision to stop such a treatment is as easy or as hard as
the decision not to start it. The moralist sees no obligation to
continue a treatment which was judged ordinary when initiated
but becomes extraordinary as the condition of the patient wors-
ens. For example, dialysis which was begun as ordinary means to
help a patient through a crisis can become extraordinary means
when dialysis becomes a way of life. Terminating the use of
extraordinary means, like "pulling the plug" on the respirator, is
not considered an act of commission causing death. In such an
instance, the patient's death is caused by that which would have
brought on death if the respirator would not have been used in
the first place.

The third difference Ramsey cites is that moralists appeal to
broader considerations than doctors do when judging ordinary
and extraordinary means. A procedure that is medically ordinary
because of the physical condition of the patient can be extraordinary in the moral sense because of the burden it places on the
patient or the minimal benefit it brings. To make a proper judgment as to whether a treatment is morally ordinary or extraordinary, we need to know more than the medical condition of the
patient. We need to know the patient's value history, perspective
on life and its meaning, the kind of life the patient has lived and
will live, and the relational character of the patient's life. What
might be a simple inconvenience for one person might be a grave
burden for someone else. On this basis, the decision as to whether
a particular means is ordinary or extraordinary belongs to the
patient. Only the patient can gauge the burden and benefit and
judge whether they are reasonable to bear. We will see more of
this issue in the fourth chapter under the discussion of "Who
Decides?"

Fluids and Nutrition: A Test Case for the Distinction

We seem to have a widespread consensus in the medical, moral and judicial communities that certain life-sustaining treatments, like the use of respirators and dialysis, which would bring no benefit to the patient but would only be a great burden can be withheld or withdrawn. However, we do not yet have this same consensus with regard to fluids and nutrition. Providing food and water is such a basic form of caring for human life. Withholding or withdrawing these carries significant symbolic meaning of that care and evokes an array of human emotions. Consequently, we cannot as easily see food and water being an optional means of treatment in the way we can see respirators and dialysis machines being optional. Yet the question remains: Can something as basic as fluids and nutrition ever be considered "extraordinary" so that it may be morally permissible to withhold or withdraw them? Trying to answer this question has become a real test case for the ordinary and extraordinary distinction, and a clear illustration of the difference between the medical and moral meaning of these terms. Several attempts have been made to address this issue.

This issue was made popular by the Clarence Herbert case in 1981. Clarence Herbert was a fifty-five year old security guard who suffered a massive loss of oxygen to his brain while recovering from uneventful surgery to remove a colostomy bag. A respirator restored his breathing, but the lack of oxygen caused severe brain damage. He was in a coma, but was not brain dead. After a short period of time, the family requested the respirator to be removed. The respirator was removed, but like Karen Quinlan, Mr. Herbert began to breathe on his own. His recovery was uncertain. Mrs. Herbert, along with other family members, authorized the withdrawal of all life-support systems, including intravenous fluids and feeding tubes. However, ordinary nursing care continued. Mr. Herbert died six days later. The withdrawal of fluids and nutrition occasioned legal prosecution. The district attorney of Los Angeles charged the two physicians, Drs. Nejdl and Barber, with murder by deprivation of medical treatment. A trial was never held in this case, though the charges of murder were reviewed by a lower court. After a hearing, the charges were dismissed. A second court reinstated the charges on the basis that the statutory definition of homicide in California was met by the circumstances of this case. But the state court of appeals again dismissed the charges, stating that the homicide definition was not fulfilled. Sufficient witnesses testified that Mr. Herbert did not have a likely chance to recover and that the proximate cause of death was the lack of oxygen to the brain, not the removal of fluids and nutrition. The judgment in this case was that fluids and nutrition were extraordinary means and could legitimately be removed. The district attorney did not appeal the decision and so the case is closed.

Another case, Infant Doe of Bloomington, Indiana, drew public attention in 1982 when this infant who had tracheoesophageal fistula and Down's Syndrome was not treated or fed. As a result of this case, the federal government intervened with the famous "Baby Doe Hotline" to ensure that such infants would be fed in the future. While the Baby Doe regulations have since been revised, the question this case raised still lingers: "Could there ever be an adequate reason to deny nutrition and fluids?"

In 1983 Claire Conroy, an eighty-four year old mentally incompetent, gravely ill woman in a New Jersey nursing home, became another public figure around this issue. She suffered from severe organic brain syndrome, gangrene, arteriosclerotic heart disease, hypertension, diabetes, necrotic decubitus ulcers and urinary tract infection. She could not speak, was confined to bed, and her ability to swallow was so limited that she had to be fed by a nasogastric tube. Though incompetent, she was not comatose nor was she diagnosed as terminally ill.

Her nephew and guardian requested her feeding tube to be removed. This request was challenged in a lower court, but the request was upheld. This decision was appealed. While the appeal was pending, Claire Conroy died with the nasogastric tube intact. The Appellate Division of the New Jersey Supreme Court decided to hear the case anyway since its issues were of significant public importance. The appellate court reversed the lower court's ruling. The appellate court ruled against withdrawal of the feeding tube since Miss Conroy was not comatose, was not being maintained by life-support machinery, and was not facing imminent death. This court judged that removing the feeding tube in her case would be equivalent to killing her since her death would not be the result of her existing medical conditions, but her death would result from introducing a new condition—dehydration and starvation.

Miss Conroy's nephew took this question to the New Jersey Supreme Court. This court released its decision on January 17, 1985 (Matter of Conroy 486 A.2d 1290) reversing the appellate court's ruling that withdrawing nutrition and fluids in this case would be killing. The New Jersey Supreme Court, like the Los Angeles Superior Court in the Clarence Herbert case, regarded artificial feeding in this instance to be a medical procedure equivalent to artificial breathing by a respirator. In other words, artificial nutrition is a medical procedure subject to the burden-benefit criteria applicable to other medical procedures.

These are only three cases which received public attention in recent years and have sparked a discussion around the issue of whether fluids and nutrition could ever be regarded as extraordinary means. Quite traditional authors of Catholic medical ethics, like Gerald Kelly,[59] Edwin Healy[60] and Charles McFadden,[61] have allowed the cessation of intravenous fluids and nutrition in instances of irreversible coma and when artificial nutrition and fluids would only prolong the final stage of dying, or become a permanent means of sustaining life. Another clear Catholic voice is heard through the National Conference of Catholic Bishops' Committee for Pro-Life Activities. In November 1984, the NCCB Administrative Committee approved for publication the Pro-Life Committee's "Guidelines for Legislation on Life-Sustaining Treatment." Guideline "h" reads:

> Recognize the presumption that certain basic measures such as nursing care, hydration, nourishment, and the like must be maintained out of respect for the human dignity of every patient.[62]

This rendering of a "presumption" in favor of providing nutrition and fluids leaves an opening to some instances wherein this presumption would give way to withholding or withdrawing

fluids and nutrition because they would not be in the best interests of the patient.

The President's Commission takes a similar position when
discussing treatment plans for patients with permanent loss of
consciousness. The commission recognizes that the only benefit
of providing artificial feeding interventions to a permanently
comatose patient is to sustain the body in the hope of the remote
possibility of recovery. The commission then adds that the sen-
sitivities of the family and care-givers ought to determine
whether these interventions ought to continue.[63]

Dr. Sidney Wanzer and his physician colleagues, writing on
the physician's responsibility toward hopelessly ill patients, sug-
gest that when a patient's disease process has reached the stage
where treatment goals are to provide only comfort care, then
"naturally or artificially administered hydration and nutrition
may be given or withheld, depending on the patient's comfort."[64]
This ought to be done, however, only with great sensitivity to the
symbolic meaning of this step and its impact on family, friends
and staff. Wanzer and his colleagues then go on to say that for
patients in a persistent vegetative state, "it is morally justifiable
to withhold antibiotics and artificial nutrition and hydration, as
well as other forms of life-sustaining treatment, allowing the
patient to die."[65]

In a more detailed study of this issue, James Childress, a professor of religious studies at the University of Virginia, and
Joanne Lynn, a physician at George Washington University,
affirm that adequate nutrition and fluids are a high priority for
most patients, but not for all.[66] They give three kinds of situations
in which food and water may be withheld because the patient in
these instances has no capacity to benefit from this care. One is
when efforts to improve fluid and nutritional balance would be
futile. This may occur in instances of patients with near total
body burn or with congestive heart failure and cancer of the
stomach with a fistula that delivers food directly to the colon
without passing through the small intestines to be absorbed into
the body. In these instances, offering food and water would bring
no benefit to a patient who is likely to die very soon. Another
situation would be the instance of anencephalic infants, or any

patient with a permanent loss of consciousness. In these cases, Carson Strong would agree with Childress and Lynn that medical interventions of any sort, even providing fluids and nutrition, would have no possibility of bringing benefit.[67] A third situation is when nutritional and fluid balance could be restored but only with severe burden for the patient. This would include those whose need for mechanical means of nutrition and fluids arises near the time of death and is accompanied by terminal pulmonary edema, nausea and mental confusion. Also included in this third group are those who are severely demented and must be restrained in order to be fed, and for whom the restraints are a constant source of fear, struggle and discomfort. In such instances, physicians David Watts and Christine Cassell would agree with Childress and Lynn that providing fluids and nutrition is extraordinary life support.[68]

Childress and Lynn draw a limited conclusion. While patients, or their proxies, may morally decide to forego nutrition and fluids in some instances, patients will be best served by providing food and fluids in most instances. Childress and Lynn give the presumption in favor of providing fluids and nutrition. However, when providing fluids and nutrition would bring no benefit to improve the clinical status of the patient, or would become too burdensome so as to cause discomfort for the patient, then fluids and nutrition may be withheld or withdrawn. For Childress and Lynn, "medical nutrition and hydration do not appear to be distinguishable in any morally relevant way from other life-sustaining medical treatments that may on occasion be withheld or withdrawn."[69]

Opposing opinions have been expressed by Daniel Callahan of the Hastings Center[70] and Gilbert Meilaender of Oberlin College.[71] Daniel Callahan argues from moral sentiment. While he can accept rationally the moral rightness of discontinuing intravenous fluids and nutrition under some circumstances (such as those identified by Childress and Lynn), a stubborn emotional repugnance keeps him from endorsing it as a moral policy. For Callahan, to withhold nutrition and fluids attacks the most fundamental of all human relationships. Providing food and drink is a basic moral obligation flowing from the fact that human life is inescapably communal. Can this conflict between the head (with its acceptance of the rational arguments supporting discontinuance of fluids and nutrition under some circumstances) and the heart (with its emotional repugnance to this kind of policy) ever be resolved? Callahan resolves it in favor of the heart by arguing that tampering with such a basic moral emotion as the revulsion at stopping feeding even under legitimate circumstances is too dangerous:

> I see no social disaster in the offing if there remains a deep-seated revulsion at the stopping of feeding even under legitimate circumstances. No doubt some people will live on in ways beneficial neither to them nor to others. No doubt a good bit of money will be wasted indulging rationally hard-to-defend anti-starvation policies. That strikes me as a tolerable price to pay to preserve—with ample margin to spare—one of the few moral emotions that could just as easily be called a necessary social instinct.[72]

Meilaender argues both from the symbolic role of providing food and water as part of human caring and from the moral conviction that it is wrong to aim to kill the innocent. The symbolic nature of providing fluids and nutrition makes regarding it as a form of medical treatment and placing it into an appraisal of a patient's medical needs very difficult. For Meilaender, providing food and drink is the sort of care all humans owe each other. In caring for the sick and dying, providing food and fluids carries the symbolic meaning of standing by those who are not yet dead as evidence that we are willing to love to the very point of death. For this reason, he disagrees with Childress and Lynn who would consider providing food and water as a form of medical care.

Moreover, fluids and nutrition by themselves do not cure. Therefore, withdrawing them is really withdrawing from an illness and allowing the patient to die. Fluids and nutrition cannot be put on the same plane as respirators, for example. If we take a patient from a respirator, the patient may die, or the patient may go on breathing spontaneously. To remove a patient from a respirator is not to aim at death, since no one smothers the patient who continues to breathe spontaneously. But if we take food and drink away from a patient, the patient will surely die. For this reason, Meilaender finds it hard to claim that we are not aiming at death when we remove food and fluids. Therefore, for him, withholding or withdrawing foods and fluid is more than allowing the patient to die. It is aiming to kill. On this basis he agrees with Callahan's assessment that the issue of providing fluids and nutrition has emerged with such vigor because "a denial of nutrition may in the long run become the only effective way to make certain that a large number of biologically tenacious patients actually die."[73]

Meilaender draws three conclusions. First, the permanently unconscious cannot experience providing fluids and nutrition as a burden, so the argument based on burden does not apply. Nor does the argument based on benefit apply since fluids and nutrition are useful to sustain the life of the non-dying, though comatose patient. Second, providing fluids and nutrition may be a burden to the conscious though severely demented patient, but fluids and nutrition are not useless. If the burden is too great, judged after a reasonable period of time, then the fluids and nutrition can be withdrawn to relieve the burden, even though death ensues as a foreseeable but unwanted side-effect. Third, for both sorts of patients, providing fluids and nutrition is not providing medical treatment in the strict sense because everyone needs food and drink to live. Stopping food and drink can only mean certain death, a death at which we can only be said to aim.[74]

These positions represent the range of opinions one is likely to encounter in the discussion on providing fluids and nutrition to the dying. Childress and Lynn provide a well-reasoned position that is in line with the traditional Roman Catholic understanding and use of the ordinary/extraordinary distinction. Callahan, however, has rightly framed the question as a struggle between the head and the heart. Sound moral principles and logical consistency are not enough to work out an adequate approach to caring for the dying. The whole person must be involved in both the care-giver as well as in those receiving care. Meilaender has rightly highlighted the symbolic role of providing nutrition and fluids as an expression of basic human care.

Richard A. McCormick has distilled several key issues from this discussion.[75] (1) One is the ambiguity of the notion "the dying patient." We cannot always clearly tell whether the patient is dying or not since "dying" is often relative to the technology available. Without access to respirators, dialysis or artificial nutrition, some patients would be clearly dying. But with such technology, these patients may not be considered "dying." (2) A second issue is the way we regard artificial hydration and nutrition. Is it a medical procedure or a basic form of human care? On the one hand, providing food and drink has enormous symbolic importance in human relationships as a basic form of human care. On the other hand, providing artificial fluids and nutrition is more like a medical procedure since it is instituted by skilled medical practitioners to compensate for impaired physical functions and carries inherent risks and possible side-effects. Furthermore, to speak of "feeding the hungry and thirsty" when we are dealing with patients who cannot take food in the normal way only confuses the issue further. (3) The third issue is the intention of death. Is withdrawing nutrition aiming at death? This depends on whether we are dealing with a dying patient whose condition prevents normal intake of food and whether providing artificial nutrition is a medical procedure or not. (4) The fourth issue is estimating burdens and benefits. Any medical treatment which imposes a greater burden than benefit is not morally required. Prolonging life by artificial nutrition is not necessarily benefiting the patient whose physical survival depends on the permanent use of artificial feeding.

McCormick concludes with his own opinion and a word of caution.

> My own opinion on these issues is that the permanently comatose and *some* noncomatose but elderly incompetent patients may be classified broadly as dying; that feeding by I.V. lines and nasogastric tubes is a medical procedure; that its discontinuance need not involve aiming at the death of such patients; and that the burden-benefit calculus may include, indeed often unavoidably includes, a quality-of-life ingredient, providing we draw the line at the right place.[76]

His word of caution recognizes that the potential for abusing the patient's best interests is great when considering withholding or withdrawing artificial nutrition. Therefore, we need to draw our lines very carefully and with clear criteria. Whenever we are uncertain about what is best, we should choose in favor of preserving life by giving greater weight to our known instinct for survival.

The discussion of the ordinary/extraordinary distinction, especially when it pertains to fluids and nutrition, highlights the need for our moral imaginations to be engaged in order to bring together head and heart in a vision of the meaning of life, the meaning of death, and the meaning of our responsibility to care for the weak and the dying.

Alternative Renderings of the Ordinary/Extraordinary Distinction

Though the ordinary/extraordinary distinction continues to be used to address these hard cases, an evaluation of the adequacy and practical clarity of these terms continues. For instance, the Vatican *Declaration on Euthanasia* follows the traditional Catholic affirmation underlying these terms that no one is obliged to use a remedy which is too burdensome or brings no benefit. However, it recognizes the difficulty with these traditional terms and cites with evident approval an alternative distinction between "proportionate" and "disproportionate" means of treatment.

Similarly, the President's Commission believes that public discussions of appropriate therapy would be clearer if the focus were on the underlying reasons for or against the therapy rather than on whether the therapy is categorized as ordinary or extraordinary. The commission recommends that policy statements and guidelines avoid these categories and speak, rather, of proportionate and disproportionate care.[77] Albert Jonsen's commentary on these terms as they are used in the commission's report shows that they express the benefit and burden of the treatment from the patient's point of view better than the terms "ordinary" and "extraordinary" do. "Proportionate" and "disproportionate" focus more clearly that the real issue at stake is not the relation of treatment to its medical effects, but the relation of treatment to the patient's capacity to appreciate the effects as a burden or a benefit.[78]

John Connery, however, finds the traditional language still helpful if properly understood. A proper understanding would keep benefit separate from burden because these notions deal with different issues and apply to different kinds of cases. He argues that "burden" is decisive for determining whether a means is obligatory or not. "Benefit" is decisive only in terminal cases.[79] However, the distinction is not limited to terminal cases. Connery's insistence on "burden" over "benefit" is to keep the duty to preserve life focused on the nature of the means needed to preserve it, and not on any quality-of-life considerations. Hence, Connery would regard means to prolong life as a "benefit" unless the patient were so near death that no available means would reasonably make a difference. Otherwise, the real issue for Connery is whether the means is too burdensome.[80]

Richard McCormick disagrees. He sees the traditional use of the ordinary/extraordinary distinction to be a way of summarizing the two basic value judgments of burden and benefit to the patient. McCormick believes that quality-of-life considerations are already packed into this distinction and are often the decisive considerations in the way these terms are used. Unlike Connery, McCormick believes that burden and benefit do not deal with different issues, but deal precisely with the core issue, quality-of-life. As he says,

> Thus, in the case of a comatose terminal-cancer patient, it has been concluded that artificial life-sustainers such as oxygen and intravenous feeding need not be used *because there is no reasonable hope of benefit for the patient,* not because there would be grave hardship in obtaining or using these supports.
>
> Once one grants that in such instances artificial life-sustainers could actually prolong the physical life of the patient (for a day, two days, a week, etc.) and yet that there is no reasonable hope of benefit for the patient (he stands to gain nothing), it is clear that one is talking about the *kind of life* the patient would have in those remaining days or weeks. This is, in my judg-

ment, a quality-of-life statement. And it has been decisive in determining whether oxygen is ordinary or extraordinary.[81]

McCormick's quality-of-life proposal is an effort to bring the formal sanctity-of-life principle into the practical arena of decision-making. Quality-of-life judgments are an extension of respect for the sanctity of life.[82] His proposal makes "the kind of life" that will be preserved one of the objective conditions of the patient that ought to be considered in determining whether treatment ought to be used. With this, the value judgment of burden and benefit shifts from focusing on the treatment to focusing on the kind of physical life the patient will have as a result of treatment.

He also shows how this standard works when dealing with the hard choices surrounding the question of prolonging life for seriously handicapped newborns. In the case of newborns, where we have no life history from which to judge perspectives on life, values and aspirations, the decisions about life-prolonging procedures ought to follow the strictest possible criteria. Richard McCormick has proposed "the potential for human relationships" as a basic criterion. According to this criterion, when the potential for human experiencing or relationships is totally absent (as in anencephalic newborns) or, because of the condition of the baby, would be totally subordinated to the mere effort for survival (as in grossly malformed newborns), then life-prolonging measures would be extraordinary and need not be taken.[83]

Paul Ramsey, however, disagrees. He rejects any quality-of-life evaluations of the patient's condition as the way to interpret what constitutes ordinary/extraordinary means. Ramsey argues that the significant moral meaning of this distinction "can be reduced almost without significant remainder to a medical indications policy."[84] Simply put, this policy says that if treatment is medically indicated it is obligatory. This policy applies to the non-dying and the dying, to the conscious and unconscious. In the case of the dying, if no further curative treatment is indicated, none is required. But in the case of the non-dying, if treatment is medically indicated, the patient cannot morally refuse it. In short, this policy leads to overriding the patient's autonomous decisions to refuse treatment if that refusal would lead to death.

It also requires providing any medically indicated therapy necessary to sustain life. Ramsey believes that such a policy directs attention to the objective medical situation of the patient's present condition and to the available medical remedies. This avoids any appeal to the subjective wishes of any of the parties concerned or to quality-of-life considerations. In this way, Ramsey disagrees not only with McCormick but also with the "reasonable person standard" of Robert Veatch.

Robert Veatch wants to respect the patient's perspective and the patient's right to refuse treatment. He thinks this can be done by translating the ordinary/extraordinary distinction into the language of reasonableness. In this way, he comes closer to McCormick's rendering of this distinction than to Ramsey's. However, what constitutes the moral meaning of "reasonable," and who decides what is "reasonable"? Veatch leaves the judgment of what is reasonable to the judgment of the one refusing the treatment. For the incompetent patient, such as the child, senile, comatose, or mentally incompetent, the proxy refusal of treatment is morally acceptable if the refusal "would seem within the realm of reason to reasonable people."[85] With this "reasonable person standard" Veatch stands in opposition to Ramsey's "medical indications policy" and believes he has preserved the meaning and wisdom of the ordinary/extraordinary distinction without getting caught in the ambiguity of the terms.

As this survey of interpretations shows, ordinary and extraordinary are not fixed categories from a moral point of view. They do not settle what we ought to do in matters pertaining to prolonging life. What we ought to do remains a prudential judgment subject to specific circumstances which can change, or which can be interpreted differently by people of good will. This distinction does, however, enshrine the wisdom that says "enough is enough" when no benefit to the patient can be achieved. The way this distinction is respected and figures into positions that have been taken on euthanasia will be evident in the next chapter.

3
The Moral Positions

Introduction

In this chapter, I will briefly synopsize ten positions which have appeared in the literature on euthanasia. I have selected those which seem to have attained relatively wide attention in discussions of euthanasia. The non-inclusion of any particular position is due simply to the fact that some limits had to be set for this chapter.

The positions surveyed in this chapter occupy a continuum between the polarities of what are called the teleological and deontological theories of moral reasoning. Teleology and deontology are large umbrella terms which cover different ways of moral reasoning.[1] A teleological theory narrowly construed yields a one-sided consequentialism. This means we can determine what is right or wrong on the basis of consequences alone, i.e., on the basis of producing the greatest possible balance of good over evil. This is sometimes called "strict consequentialism." A teleological theory more broadly conceived, however, determines the morality of actions on the basis of the total meaning of the action. All aspects of the action (such as what is being sought, what means are used, in what circumstances) and not just consequences must be seen in their proper relationship in orde to determine the true moral object and to make a proper moral judgment. This form of teleology is sometimes called "mixed consequentialism." Deontological theories, on the other hand, hold that at least some acts are wrong and others are right independent of their consequences. Duties and rules generally prescribe these right-making and wrong-making characteristics.

I will organize the positions on euthanasia according to three distinguishable groups along the continuum from teleology to deontology. I will begin with an extreme teleological position and move progressively to the opposite extreme in deontology. This organization follows the schema I used in my chapter on theories of material moral norms in my other book in this series, *What Are They Saying About Moral Norms?*[2] Organizing the discussion on euthanasia according to these prominent theories in normative ethics for interpreting principles and making moral judgments helps to show that issues in medical ethics are an application of the work going on in philosophical and religious ethics. Furthermore, organizing the positions this way also shows that much of the controversy over euthanasia can be explained as a matter of conflicting philosophical and theological presuppositions and ethical methods. In my synopses, I try to reflect both the presuppositions and the method of each position.

In brief, then, this chapter proceeds along the following pattern. The first group represents the teleological position of strict consequentialism proposed by Joseph Fletcher and Marvin Kohl. This approach holds that the moral rightness of all actions is determined solely by the consequences. The second group represents the teleological position of mixed consequentialism. Daniel C. Maguire, Charles E. Curran, and Richard A. McCormick represent the wide spectrum of this middle position. It holds that consequences play an important but not the sole role in determining the moral rightness of an action. The third group represents the deontological approach. Paul Ramsey, the Vatican *Declaration on Euthanasia,* Germain Grisez, Joseph M. Boyle, Jr., William E. May, Arthur J. Dyck and vitalism represent this position. It maintains that some actions have right-making and wrong-making characteristics independently of consequences.

Strict Consequentialist Positions

With regard to euthanasia, a strict consequentialist takes the moral stance that life is a basic, but not an absolute good. In this position, one's moral posture before human life is to respect life and generally not to take direct action against it. But in some circumstances, the strict consequentialist would consider the direct termination of one's own life or another's to be morally permissible as the most loving and kind thing to do.

Joseph Fletcher

Joseph Fletcher, an Episcopalian priest and professor of biomedical ethics at the University of Virginia School of Medicine, is well known for his celebrated *Situation Ethics: The New Morality*.[3] Throughout his career Fletcher has managed to remain controversial and a bit polemical in his style. Right or wrong, he always provokes. His approach to the moral rightness of actions is his version of "situationalism." It is well summarized in these few sentences:

> *Christian* situation ethics has only one norm or principle of law (call it what you will) that is binding and unexceptional, always good and right regardless of the circumstances. That is "love"—the *agape* of the summary commandment to love God and the neighbor. Everything else without exception, all laws and rules and principles and ideals and norms, are only *contingent,* and only valid *if they happen* to serve love in any situation.[4]

His conclusions with regard to euthanasia are based on the requirements of love in relation to the needs of dying patients.

Fletcher's first book in medical ethics, *Morals and Medicine* (1954),[5] espouses this approach to decision-making which lets the context and consequences, not a fixed set of rules, be decisive. This approach attracts those who want to emphasize the importance of moral flexibility and who want to respect the idiosyncrasy of individual clinical cases. Fletcher's subsequent writings in medical ethics have consistently defended the right to take one's own life or another's for compassionate reasons and as a way of protecting human dignity. Fletcher defends his position in basically three steps.

First, his position is an aggressive attack on the doctrine of vitalism, which represents the totally opposite extreme of his own position. He feels that the greatest obstacle to compassionate ending of life is the vitalistic fallacy that thinks death ought to be natural—humanly uncontrolled and uncontrived.[6] Yet for Fletcher, intelligent control over physical nature, such as in controlling birth as well as in controlling death, is a right of spiritual beings and a matter of human dignity.

Religiously put, the vitalistic fallacy leaves life "in God's hands." God reserves the right to decide at what moment life shall cease. But Fletcher wants us to rid ourselves of this archaic theodicy according to which God is the cause, builder and manager of nature. Such a view assumes that God's will is revealed in what nature does, and that physiological life as such is sacrosanct and untouchable. Fletcher favors understanding God as the creative principle behind everything so that medicine is truly and rightly "playing God" when it intervenes to prolong life or end life when circumstances warrant.[7]

He challenges vitalism's contention that life as such is the highest good. Such thoroughgoing vitalism is "more loyal to the physical spark of mere biological life than to the personality values of self-possession and human integrity."[8] From his personalistic view which puts humanness and personal integrity above biological life and function, Fletcher places the highest good in personal integrity and human well-being. As he says,

> It is *personal* function that counts, not biological function. Humanness is understood as primarily rational, not physiological. This "doctrine of man" puts the *homo* and *ratio* before the *vita*. It holds that being human is more "valuable" than being alive.[9]

By "personal function" and "being human" he means cerebration, i.e., the function of the cerebral cortex. The core of humanness lies in the rational faculty. With the loss of cerebral function (the synthesizing "mind"),

> the *person* is gone (dead) no matter how many other spontaneous or artificially supported functions persist in the heart, lungs, and vascular system. Such noncerebral processes might as well be turned off, whether they are natural or artificial.[10]

Fletcher's argument against vitalism, then, emphasizes cerebration. When the cerebral cortex ceases to function, only subhuman life remains.

Second, Fletcher argues for the moral identity between deliberately allowing the dying patient to die and deliberately causing the dying patient to die. The intention is the same, either way. So is the consequence.

> It is naive and superficial to suppose that because we don't "do anything positively" to hasten a patient's death we have thereby avoided complicity in his death. Not doing anything is doing something; it is a decision to act every bit as much as deciding for any other deed.[11]

For Fletcher the distinction between omission and commission is merely descriptive. It provides a practical distinction for understanding human actions. But it does not designate a moral difference in human activity.

In his earlier writing, Fletcher distinguished direct (active/positive) and indirect (passive/negative) forms of euthanasia. He reserved the term "euthanasia" for directly inducing death to end incurable suffering. But since many found "euthanasia" psychologically difficult to bear and because the law had not yet caught up with what he regarded as morally right behavior, Fletcher began to use the term "anti-dysthanasia" to mean the refusal to prolong a painful condition in all patients except those who specifically expressed opposition to hastening their death. He thought that this could be an intermediate step in securing general acceptance of direct euthanasia. Anti-dysthanasia could be administered in any of three forms: (1) giving a pain relieving drug which would reduce suffering but also hasten death; (2) pulling the plugs on life support systems; (3) withholding CPR.[12]

In his more recent writing, however, he clearly defends direct euthanasia and has abandoned his use of anti-dysthanasia. He now considers the issue of negative euthanasia (anti-dysthanasia) to be settled. He sees it as an accomplished fact in modern medicine. For Fletcher, "arguing pro and con about negative euthanasia is therefore merely flogging a dead horse."[13] In fact,

Fletcher now so strongly favors direct euthanasia for a life enmeshed in incurable and fatal physical suffering that he believes "it is harder morally to justify letting somebody die a slow and ugly death, dehumanized, than it is to justify helping him to escape from such misery."[14] However, Fletcher does not advocate eugenic euthanasia for those who are a burden on the community.[15]

Third, the crux of Fletcher's situationalism lies in his way of relating means to ends in order to achieve what love requires. The heart of his love ethics is "getting results" here and now. If the consequences are good, the actions causing them are good. Though Fletcher holds that the end justifies the means, he does not hold that any end will justify any means. The end must be a good proportionate to the means. Arguing that the highest good or end is human happiness and personal well-being, he concludes that in some tragic circumstances suicide or mercy killing can be exactly what is called for in order to validate the happiness and well-being of persons.[16]

For Fletcher, then, love requires that we seek the greatest good for ourselves and others. In some instances, this love requires the direct termination of life, one's own or another's, in order to ensure the personal integrity, human well-being and happiness of persons.

Marvin Kohl

Marvin Kohl, an analytic philosopher at the State University of New York College at Fredonia, represents a non-theistic view of making a case for voluntary active euthanasia. He states his claim forthrightly: "My claim is that in situations where there are no overriding rights or similar considerations voluntary active euthanasia . . . is a moral obligation."[17] He speaks of the euthanasia which he regards as a moral obligation as "beneficent" since it satisfies the love ethic's principle of beneficence which sees mercy killing as the kindest possible treatment of an unfortunate person.

Kohl's most complete argument for beneficent euthanasia is in his book of essays, *The Morality of Killing* (1974).[18] Here we find his threefold argument. He argues first against a vitalistic ethic and for a love ethic with its concomitant rule of benevolence. Then he argues from kindness, and lastly from justice.

He develops his basic perspective by taking a stand against vitalism and its absolute rendition of the sanctity of life principle. He realizes that the question of the morality of euthanasia is not likely to arise unless one already believes that continuing mere physical life is an absolute and intrinsic good. But Kohl does not believe that this vitalistic position can stand. It tolerates unnecessary suffering which is not a virtue, it runs counter to the common moral intuition of beliefs about killing in self-defense, and it flies in the face of the general moral approval of heroes, heroines, and martyrs. Kohl examines and finds wanting the absolute claim of the sanctity of life principle (namely, "one ought never to kill an innocent human being"). He proposes a reformulation which is in line with the complexity of moral experience: "Generally speaking, one ought not to kill a human being whose existence or actions neither have caused nor will cause imminent harm."[19] Against the posture of vitalism, he upholds a love ethic with its concomitant rule of benevolence to maintain that sometimes killing is the kindest deed to perform.

Accompanying the rule of benevolence in Kohl's analysis is the rule of beneficence which provides the moral foundation for his major argument from kindness. His major premise is that beneficence entails the obligation to act kindly toward one another. He specifies the sense in which an act can be described as kind:

> An act is kind if it (a) is intended to be helpful; (b) is done so that, if there be any expectation of receiving remuneration (or the like), the individual would nonetheless act even if it became apparent that there was little chance of his expectation being realized; and (c) results in beneficial treatment for the intended recipient. The Boy or Girl Scout helping an elderly man or woman across the street, and the proverbial Good Samaritan, are paradigm cases of kindness.[20]

From this understanding of kindness he can draw his minor premise that euthanasia is "beneficent," or an act of kindness, if it

(i) results in the painless inducement of a quick death; (ii) results (i.e., the act as a whole) in beneficial treatment for the intended recipient; (iii) is intended to be helpful; and (iv) is done so that, if there is any expectation of receiving remuneration (or the like), the individual would still act in that manner, even if it becomes apparent that there is little or no chance of his expectation being realized.[21]

To clarify further what he means by "beneficent euthanasia," he offers two paradigm cases. The first involves (1) a patient suffering from an irremediable condition of cancer; (2) the patient is in excruciating pain; (3) beyond reasonable medical doubt, the patient will die as a result of this condition; (4) when told of his condition, the patient voluntarily favors an "easy death"; (5) aside from the desire to help the patient, no other conditions are relevant. The second type of case occurs in instances such as when (1) a child is born without limbs, sight, hearing, or a functioning cerebral cortex; (2) the child is suffering no pain; (3) death is not imminent; (4) aside from the desire to help the patient, no other conditions are relevant.

These different cases share two features: Both involve serious and irremediable physical conditions, and the motivation in both is the desire to help. Kohl judges that induced death in each case would be viewed by most people as an act of kindness.[22] With these paradigms in mind, and on the assumption that we are obliged to act kindly, he concludes that beneficent euthanasia (because it is an act of kindness) is a moral obligation and should be made a rule of practice.

His argument from justice is that we give to each according to his or her basic needs. Justice requires that we meet the need for self-respect by ensuring informed consent. Where a person is free to choose, consent is necessary. This is the best defense of justice. Secondly, all have the need for dignity and to be so treated. Therefore, justice requires that we respect the dignity of the person. "Dignity" is elusive. By "dignity" Kohl means the ability rationally to determine and control one's life and death. Dignity also extends to having this ability respected by others.[23] But Kohl does not want to restrict euthanasia only to cases where consent can be obtained. Sometimes the person is not being served when his or her misery is increasing and consent is not possible. Neither justice nor the person is being served by prolonging suffering simply because the patient cannot give consent to end it.[24]

Kohl's position, then, like Fletcher's, emphasizes the supremacy of personal values such as freedom and dignity to be greater than the value of physical life alone. Whereas Fletcher argued from the imperative of love, Kohl adds arguments from kindness and justice. Actions destructive of physical life not only can be morally justified if they are acts of kindness and justice promoting the dignity of the person, but for Kohl they would be morally required. But killing is kind for Kohl only under limited circumstances and as a last resort. He does not advocate euthanasia for economic purposes. He aims to minimize suffering and maximize kindness in our efforts to preserve the dignity of human beings.

Strict Consequentialist Positions: An Assessment

After reviewing these representatives of a strict consequentialist position, certain strengths and weaknesses stand out. Some of its strengths are that this position is clearly motivated by compassion. It recognizes that withholding and withdrawing treatment does not automatically result in immediate death. Sometimes the dying linger in a seriously debilitated condition. Advocating euthanasia as a moral obligation helps us see that many values of life go beyond that of physical survival. This position also challenges us to consider seriously whether death is the greatest harm that we can ever undergo. Can life become so unbearable that continued living would be more harmful than death brought on by direct intervention? These strict consequentialists think so. We may not agree with this conclusion, but we cannot avoid raising the question.

Some of the weaknesses of this position are that its conclusion that killing out of love and kindness is a moral obligation remains arbitrary, it is too risky, and it erodes the character of a helping community of trust and care. It is arbitrary because its argument draws upon a few selected values that define human potential, like happiness and well-being, and it fails to set these within a full spectrum of values and consequences before validating euthanasia. For example, no place is given to the positive value of suffering in this approach.

Second, a policy of euthanasia is too risky. Even though killing for mercy seems to produce more good than harm in the short run, the net consequences of such killing may provide reasons to avoid it as a moral obligation. A policy of actively killing for mercy can set a precedent that could lead to its being applied more broadly. For example, even if permitting euthanasia in one instance does not logically justify other similar instances, wider application to the most vulnerable members of the community, such as the elderly and mentally and physically handicapped, may result from the lowering of psychological and social barriers to killing.

Moreover, the long-term effects of a policy of euthanasia could be a weakening of vigilance and carefulness on the part of those who care for the weak and the dying. It could also lead to a loss of respect for life and of trust by patients in health care professionals. Adopting a policy of euthanasia can easily impede one's imagination to explore a wider range of alternatives such as forms of support care, like hospice, or alternative means of financial assistance. It may also make one less sensitive to what a patient really wants when asking to die. Also, the possibility of the abuse of such a policy by persons not of good faith is ever present. The risk of such detrimental long-term consequences to potential victims as well as to the health care professional outweighs the advantages of adopting a policy of euthanasia for the particular patient who desires it.

Third, making euthanasia a moral obligation erodes the character of a helping community of trust and care. If we focused our attention exclusively on the dying patient and extended our vision no farther, then perhaps we might be able to make a good case for euthanasia. But if we are socially conscious so that our vision encompasses the caring community as well, then we can make a better case against euthanasia. The sort of community we are and are going to be is reflected in our way of caring for the dying. This social focus on our care for the dying is another criticism against a policy of euthanasia.

Stanley Hauerwas has provided a critical perspective along these lines in his approach to an ethics of care for the dying. For him the real issue is not whether euthanasia ought to be a moral obligation or not. The real issue is the sort of community of trust and care we ought to be in order to see death as an ending we need not hasten.[25] As Hauerwas sees it, we exist and are sustained by communities of trust and care. In fact, he says, one of the reasons for prohibiting euthanasia is to show the one who is dying "the continuing trustworthiness of his or her existence."[26] Euthanasia threatens the trust that must prevail between us if we are to live a human life at all. Hauerwas argues that whether and how we decide to care for the dying does not depend on whether the dying person has passed the line from cerebration to some form of subhuman life. Rather, whether and how we care depends on our perception of our role as relative, friend, or health care provider.[27] Would we not be hesitant to seek the care of another if we thought that he or she might actually eliminate our suffering by eliminating us? Killing is incompatible with our call to stand by and with one another in trust. This is especially applicable to the medical professionals whose role of healing in our society depends on trust prevailing.

Furthermore, both Fletcher and Kohl want to end suffering as kindly and painlessly as possible. We must be careful, cautions Hauerwas, to be clear whose suffering we are most concerned to end—the patient's, or ours occasioned by having to keep company with a patient whose suffering we cannot relieve.[28] To make euthanasia a moral obligation can too easily become a way of doing away with those who bother us and lead us to see a life free of suffering as the only life worth living. We ought not to look on suffering as something to be sought for its own sake, or even as something to accept as a way of gaining grace or becoming holy. Yet we ought to regard suffering not as something always to avoid, but as something with which we learn to live. If we too easily relieve suffering by elimination, then we may have nothing left to impel our imaginations to develop new forms of caring, and, perhaps, even curing. Euthanasia can be a sign that uncaring has triumphed and our imaginations have atrophied.

For reasons like these, and from a perspective like that which Stanley Hauerwas urges, a strict consequentialist approach to euthanasia can be a dangerous moral position to promote.

Mixed Consequentialist Positions

Mixed consequentialism includes a wide spectrum of possibilities. Only three will be represented here. This position avoids a one-sided consequentialism of a teleological theory narrowly conceived. The "mixed consequentialist" position does not abandon teleology, but conceives it more broadly to include the whole meaning of the action which entails the proper relation of all its aspects. This means that we need to appeal to more than consequences to claim moral objectivity and to discover the true moral meaning of an act. The fundamental moral conviction of this position is that life is a basic but not an absolute good. One is bound to respect life, but no one is obliged to prolong it in every circumstance. This position, then, allows diverse interpretations of the general rule that one should not take direct action to terminate life.

On the one extreme of the continuum of this approach is Daniel C. Maguire who holds the rule against killing to be binding unless it comes into conflict with stronger values, as it often does. Charles E. Curran, however, finds the rule only giving way to stronger values when the dying process overtakes the patient. Then direct action to terminate life becomes morally equivalent to allowing the patient to die by withdrawing or withholding life-prolonging treatment. Richard A. McCormick, even more cautiously, considers the rule to be virtually exceptionless because of the foreseeable harm that not following the rule would cause.

Daniel C. Maguire

Daniel C. Maguire, a Roman Catholic moral theologian at Marquette University, commands the attention of moralists by the way he uncovers presuppositions and re-evaluates fundamental questions often begged in long-standing positions on euthanasia.

Maguire recognizes that a momentous issue like euthanasia can be handled adequately only within the broad context of a complete ethical theory. This is what he has tried to do in *Death by Choice* (1974, updated and expanded in 1984).[29] In the second part of this book, he sketches a method for "doing" ethics. He has elaborated this method in his major book on method in ethics, *The Moral Choice* (1978).[30] For Maguire, the special task of doing ethics is to bring sensitivity, reflection and method to the way people decide the sort of persons they ought to be and the sort of actions they ought to perform. The first step in Maguire's method is to discover the moral object, i.e., the act with all its meaning-giving circumstances. He suggests that we do this by raising the reality-revealing questions—what, why, how, who, where, when, what if and what else. Once we have ascertained the moral object by asking these questions, we can turn to ways of evaluating it. This involves the use of principles, rational analysis, feelings (which he calls *Gemüt,* or what the heart knows), creative imagination, group experience, and the role of the discerning judgment of the moral subject(s) involved. Only within such a thorough investigation of the moral reality can we adequately advance an argument on an issue so complex as euthanasia. Maguire has done that in *Death by Choice* and answers "yes" to the central question of his book, "Can it be moral and should it be legal to take direct action to terminate life in certain circumstances?"[31]

In this book he explores many of the key questions raised in discussions of euthanasia, and his answers to some of these questions disclose his position. For example: Must we in all cases await the good pleasure of biochemical and organic factors and allow these to determine the time and manner of death? No. Can the will of God regarding a person's death be manifested only through the collapse of sick or wounded organs? No. Can the will of God be discovered through human sensitivity and reasoning? Yes. Could there be circumstances when it would be reasonable and therefore moral to terminate life through either positive action or calculated benign neglect? Yes.

In advancing his argument, both his faith and his philosophy become evident. His faith is evident in his rejecting a kind of theistic fatalism which would forbid expanding the human moral dominion over dying in the name of the divine prerogative of determining the end of life. Maguire challenges the theistic assumption about dominion which asserts that terminating a life is violating the property rights of God. In religious language, this assumption of theistic fatalism would read:

> When God wants you to die, your organs will fail or disease will overcome you. Organic collapse is the medium through which God's will is manifested. Positive action to accelerate death, however, would amount to wresting the matter out of God's hands and taking it into your own. It is a sin of arrogant presumption.[32]

This theistic assumption supports a physicalistic ethics which leaves us at the mercy of biochemical and organic factors to mediate God's will and to determine the time and manner of death. Maguire challenges such an assumption and the ethics it implies. If we could not intervene in nature's ways, he maintains, all medicine would be immoral.

Maguire believes that we have underestimated our dominion over life and death. His theistic preference is to see us as participators in divine providence with the prerogative and responsibility to discover the good and choose it—even when the good in question is death. This does not make the Christian community committed to death by choice. But it does show that we know whether or not a choice for death is moral from within the struggling moral community where we come to know the limits of our God-given freedom.

Maguire's philosophy is evident in his advancing the argument that terminating a life under certain circumstances may be good so long as a greater good than physical life is being served. He regards such goods as personal integrity, human dignity and the freedom of self-determination to be proportionate to the good of physical life. This position challenges the "absolute" and "exceptionless" character often given to the principle, "Thou shalt not kill," and its satellite principles, such as "Never do anything to hasten the death of a patient," and "Ordinary means must be used to preserve life." If these principles are sufficient for all complex situations of life, then any action done to hasten death is immoral. But are these principles sufficient? Maguire thinks not.

He defends his position of death by choice against the objections of the "no direct killing of innocent life" principle on the basis of his understanding of the source, function and limits of moral principles. He regards principles as indispensable for ethics since they express in propositional form a value judgment reflecting the accumulative wisdom of human experience of what helps or hinders the fulfillment of persons. Principles are born from an experience of value. The primary value underlying the principles against taking life is the value of human life. The validity of any exception to principles which try to express this value depends on the exception being able to express an equal or greater appreciation of the same primal value—the sacredness of life. This means that the principle and its exception must be good for the same reason—namely, each expresses the concrete demands of the sacredness of human life.

Maguire regards the "no direct killing of innocent life" principle to be valid most of the time, but recognizes that in the specific circumstances of the patient's moral situation, the principle may not apply and would have to yield to the principle of achieving a good death. To make the principle against mercy killing to be without exception, the consequences of such a killing would have to be so disastrous that they would outweigh all possible contending values.[33] Maguire believes that there are cases where greater values than physical life prevail. He gives some examples:

> If we decide that a patient reduced to vegetative status should be terminated, it would be because of a determination that the physical and non-moral evil of that person's *complete* death is more than compensated for by proportionate values. Among these would be: ending the macabre spectacle of maintaining a body in biological life after the personality is extinguished, ending the hopeless expense for treatment that cannot cure,

relief of a grieving family, reallocation of medical resources, etc.[34]

In advancing an argument for the moral validity of directly terminating life in some circumstances, Maguire is not condoning a passion for euthanasia. But he does recognize that it may at times be a viable moral choice.

> There should be no passion for euthanasia. Indeed we should work for the conditions which make it less and less indicated. To say this, however, does not close the door to moral mercy killing any more than favoring the conditions of peace makes one into an absolute pacifist.[35]

Unless someone holds that continued living in any condition is always preferable, he or she will have to enter into the weighing of proportional values. Maguire realizes that the long experience of the Christian moral community which lies behind the "no direct killing of the innocent" principle makes one hesitate before admitting exceptions. He also knows that making the judgment between conflicting values is not so tidy and neat as to dispel any apprehension that the judgment may not be correct. But the whole purpose of ethical reflection like that which he proposes is to achieve a finer sensitivity to the values in conflict and make possible options, even the options for life and death, less arbitrary.

For Maguire, then, the generally accepted principle against the direct termination of life always counts in one's moral evaluation but does not always win. Values such as personal dignity, freedom of self-determination, and excessive burden of expense are values which he finds proportionate to maintaining physical life and to be preferred in some instances. Therefore, euthanasia can sometimes be a legitimate moral choice. Other mixed consequentialists who judge between conflicting values can and do come to conclusions different from Maguire's.

Charles E. Curran

Charles E. Curran, of the Catholic University of America, has contributed to the discussion on euthanasia by analyzing it from the perspective of the notion of dominion and from within his relational-responsibility model of doing ethics.

The fundamental imperative to respect life is rooted in Curran's faith conviction that the sanctity of life, the dignity of life, or the value of life comes from "the special relation of the human being to the life-giving act of God and from the destiny of each person."[36] On the basis of this conviction, Curran maintains that the value of life transcends accomplishments, possessions or capacities which contemporary society often counts as essential to the value of human life. Respect for life stemming from creation is reinforced for Curran by the mystery of redemption in Christ and the biblical criterion that our love for God is expressed in our love for the neighbor in need. The Christian bias for the poor, the weak and the oppressed shows again that the ultimate value of human life comes from God's gracious gift to us and not from anything we might have done.[37]

While accepting that respect for life is based on the mystery of creation, Curran also cautions that too great a stress on life as gift can downplay the role and place of human responsibility in exercising self-determination and stewardship in a reasonable way. In making decisions about keeping human life in existence, exercising stewardship does not exclude weighing the value of life against other values, such as cost, physical and mental suffering, or freedom. Curran finds this sort of weighing of values to be a reasonable exercise of stewardship. Such weighing is already included in the Catholic tradition's acceptance of the distinction between ordinary and extraordinary means of treatment. From the point of view of dominion and the responsible exercise of stewardship over the dying process, his fundamental position on euthanasia is clear:

> I agree with the traditional argument against euthanasia, that man does not have full dominion over his life and, therefore, cannot positively interfere to take his life. . . . Man does have some dominion over the dying process because of which he can as a matter of fact shorten the time of his dying by not using or discontinuing even readily available means to prolong life.[38]

By accepting the distinction between ordinary and extraordinary means, Curran finds that the Catholic tradition does not absolutize physical life but recognizes the importance of quality of life and other values that claim attention. Also, he finds in this tradition that respect for life is not the only moral criterion to which one appeals in judgments involving human life. On this basis, he can use his relational-responsibility model of ethics to solve conflicts of values inherent in the question of euthanasia.

In applying his model to the issue of euthanasia, Curran distinguishes the theoretical basis for respecting life from the normative question of criteria for judgments made about human life. For example, without denying the mystery of creation as the basis for respecting human life, Curran finds that in a conflict where values commensurate with life are at stake, one may legitimately take a human life. This, in fact, is what the Catholic tradition has already done in seeing killing in self-defense to be reconcilable with respect for life.

> If necessary one may kill an actual unjust aggressor if this is required to save life or spiritual or material goods of great value. Note that here Catholic theologians have been willing to admit that other values, such as spiritual goods (e.g., use of reason, reputation, etc.) or material goods of great value, could be as important as physical life itself.[39]

The traditional Catholic approach to such a conflict has appealed to the principle of double effect, especially its distinction between direct and indirect effect. Curran challenges the adequacy of this distinction on the basis of the relational character of the moral act. He sees the full human act in its relationship with other values and persons as well as in their responses to the act. Therefore, in solving conflicts, he maintains that values commensurate with human life can justify taking human life. As he says, "In conflict situations in which one's life or other goods of commensurate value are being threatened, then one could be justified in taking the life of another as a last resort."[40] Curran makes his judgment on the basis of the commensurate values involved rather than on the basis of the physical integrity of the act. Therefore, he, like Maguire but unlike Grisez, Boyle and May, whom we will soon see, would allow one to act directly against some basic goods in order to save other proportionate goods.[41]

This model of solving conflicts, together with his assessment of dominion and responsible stewardship, is the context for understanding Curran's qualified stance on euthanasia. He does not find that the theistic fatalism of limited dominion, which prevents direct interference with life, is convincing once a person has begun to die. The traditional acceptance of refusing extraordinary means is evidence that we do have some dominion over life and can intend to die and effectively carry out that intention by discontinuing or refusing available means to prolong life. But once the dying process begins, the difference between omission and commission no longer holds. Therefore, he would morally support positively interfering to shorten the dying process.

With this, Curran allows positive intervention at a point earlier than Ramsey would, as we will soon see. For Curran, the moral significance of the distinction between omission and commission dissolves when the dying process overtakes a person. To intervene to kill the dying patient at this point would not be an exercise of full dominion over life, nor would it be an arrogant act of "playing God."[42]

This proposal—that the distinction between omission and commission dissolves when the dying process overtakes a person—has its practical problems. Curran wants to avoid opening the door to all sorts of euthanasia. For that reason he confines the legitimacy of positive intervention to the dying process. This will protect those who are seriously ill but not dying. But how determine when the dying process begins? Curran offers a practical guide:

> I acknowledge problems in determining when the dying process begins (some could argue it begins at birth), so I practically identify the dying process with the time that means can be discontinued as useless but having in mind such means as respirators, intravenous feeding, etc. In practice there will always be a difficulty in determining just when the dying process begins so that one must recognize the potential problem

of abuse that can arise and the difficulty in determining laws in this matter.[43]

Curran, then, accepts life as a primordial value, the sanctity of life as a basic principle, and respect for life as a moral imperative. He also accepts the traditional argument against euthanasia based on limited dominion which prevents a positive intervention to take life. However, since the dying process indicates that life has reached its limit, Curran sees no usurping of full dominion once it begins. As the patient's dying dissolves the moral distinction between omission and commission, Curran's relational-responsibility model of ethics provides a method of resolving conflicts of values so that the direct taking of life may be allowed when other values commensurate with life are present. With this reasoning, Curran gives a qualified acceptance to euthanasia in limited circumstances.

Richard A. McCormick

Richard A. McCormick, a Catholic moral theologian from the Kennedy Institute for Bioethics at Georgetown University, has won the respect of theologians of every persuasion. His perceptive analysis of moral issues and the positions of others over the years has earned him a hearing in every camp. His analysis of the arguments on euthanasia is no exception.

In approaching euthanasia, McCormick takes as a given the sanctity of life and the imperative to respect life. He also takes as a given the general prohibition to take human life. His contribution to the discussion of euthanasia lies in the form of the moral reasoning he uses to support and limit any exceptions to the general norm "Do not kill."

His method first of all recognizes that every human choice represents a resolution of conflict. In resolving conflict, every human choice inevitably fails to realize all possible values. Concrete moral norms, like "the direct killing of an innocent person is immoral," which we use to guide us through conflicts of value are specific expressions of the more general conviction that when values are in conflict, and we cannot realize all possible values, then the reasonable thing to do is to do the greater good, or avoid the greater evil. Or, in the language of the premoral evil/proportionate reason thought-pattern which has become familiar through McCormick's analyses over the past fifteen years, "we may cause or permit premoral evils only when there is a truly proportionate reason."[44] In this light, McCormick reads the traditional norms for caring for the dying to mean:

> (1) there is a proportionate reason for not using (omission) every means to save a life, or to prolong dying; (2) there is no proportionate reason for directly dispatching a terminal or dying patient.[45]

McCormick's own position becomes evident as he examines each of these propositions. He takes the first—there is a proportionate reason for not prolonging life at any cost and with every means—as commonly accepted. The implication of this proposition is that "human life is a basic good and may not be taken except where higher values are at stake and cannot be preserved in any other way."[46] To say there may be a proportionate reason not to prolong life is already to put a different evaluation on dying life than on life that is not dying. This means that the same basic value, "life," can call forth different obligations at various stages or phases of its existence. If we can claim a proportionate reason for not using all means to prolong life, then we are claiming a point where it would be to the good of the patient to allow death to occur. This recognizes that bodily existence can represent a value that may conflict with another more important and to-be-preferred value, such as personal dignity, integrity and freedom. Such an approach values life without absolutizing it, and does not try to avoid death at any cost.

McCormick then addresses the second proposition by asking this question: "Does this difference in evaluation of dying life also lead to the conclusion that irreversibly dying life may be terminated directly, that there is a proportionate reason for direct termination?"[47] He thinks not. He defends himself by recording his dissatisfaction with the two positions taken on this question.

One position argues for the immorality of the direct termination of life. This position (represented by Grisez, Boyle and

May) is based on the inherent value of life as a basic good which cannot be weighed against any other values. However, since this position would not endorse sustaining life at all costs and in any circumstances, it actually abandons its fundamental conviction that human life is a basic good incommensurate with other basic goods. It actually holds that the dying patient need not be treated in the same way as the non-dying patient. In other words, the duties to support and protect a patient while dying are different from those which are proper to supporting and protecting the non-dying patient.

On the other side are those (like Joseph Fletcher) who settle the issue by seeing no difference between omission and commission. Whatever proportionate reason could justify allowing a person to die could be used to justify ending life by positive direct intervention. This is the position which says that, at a certain point in the dying process, the moral difference between omission and commission dissolves. McCormick does not accept this position. For him the inevitability of the dying process, or the near imminence of death, does not make the manner in which a person dies morally indifferent. McCormick finds the short and long range implications and effects of actions of omission and commission to reveal the moral difference between omission and commission. As he says,

> In other words, mere omission may not entail, either logically or factually, the same consequences as direct commission would. And if this is so, a different calculus of proportion may be called for. For proportion must encompass the good of the patient and all concerned. . . . When all the values are weighed, I would tentatively suggest that what is proportionate for allowing a terminal patient to die is not proportionate for directly causing death. And if this is true, it means that omission and commission are not *morally* identical, at least insofar as the moral significance is traceable to, or revealed by, effects.[48]

Some of the effects, short and long range, would include the effect on the doctor-patient relationship, the effect on the interests of the person or persons who would be able to decide when euthanasia would be permitted, the effect on society's establishing some qualitative standards of usefulness or burdensomeness, and the effect on the quality and attitude of mercy among health-care providers.[49]

In short, McCormick holds to a moral difference between omission and commission and regards the foreseeable harms involved in the direct termination of life to be disproportionate to the benefits. On this basis, he judges it reasonable to regard the direct termination of life to be a "virtually exceptionless" norm, or a practical absolute. The risk of an alternative policy to the norm which prohibits direct killing of terminal patients seems too great.

McCormick, then, as we shall soon see, agrees with Grisez, Boyle and May that life and health are basic goods which define human well-being and give rise to our moral obligations and value commitments. However, he disagrees with the method-ological implication of this starting point. Two crucial questions of method are at stake: (1) What counts for turning against a basic good? (2) Why? Whereas Grisez, Boyle and May regard directly turning against a basic good to be intrinsically morally evil, McCormick regards it as a premoral evil needing the justification of a proportionate reason. This is a crucial difference between the two positions. For McCormick, an action can be regarded as "turning directly against a basic good" only after the relation of that choice to all values has been weighed carefully. This inevi-tably involves a balancing of goods and values which Grisez, Boyle and May do not want to make. Like Maguire and Curran, McCormick uses the thought structure of proportionality. Unlike them, however, he draws a more cautious conclusion.

Mixed Consequentialist Positions: An Assessment

This middle position takes seriously the values that come into conflict in situations surrounding the dying. To address con-flict, it follows a thought-pattern which tries to determine the morality of an action on the basis of the total meaning of the action, not just the consequences. This means that all aspects of the action must be seen in their proper relationship.

As these three positions demonstrate, each regards life as a primary value. Each regards the principle prohibiting killing to be a valid principle for protecting life. However, while each uses the same basic ethical method to interpret moral actions and apply moral principles, each yields a somewhat different assessment of the values in conflict as well as a somewhat different judgment of whether and when these values and the various aspects of actions surrounding care for the dying are properly proportionate. For example, for Maguire a merciful death can be a greater value than a prolonged life in a debilitated condition. For him the principle prohibiting killing will have to yield to the more compelling value of achieving a merciful death in order to uphold the sanctity of life. For Curran, the prohibition against killing holds firm until the dying process overtakes the person and no obligation remains to protect life. McCormick holds firm to the principle against killing as a practical absolute. He judges the net consequences of harm that would result if killing were permitted to be disproportionate to the benefit that would come.

Maguire draws the circumstances and consequences justifying euthanasia quite narrowly. For this reason, his position is subject to the same sorts of criticisms as those leveled against the strict consequentialist position. Furthermore, both Maguire and Curran appeal to the notion of dominion as a theological ground for approaching euthanasia. But, as we have already seen in the second chapter, Bruno Schüller has argued that dominion merely restates what needs to be proved in the euthanasia discussion, namely, whether anyone has the power to end life. Moreover, both Maguire and Curran are subject to the criticisms which come from the perspective of Hauerwas on active intervention in another's death as eroding the character of the caring community. Even though Curran's notion of the "dying process" results in a more restrictive position than Maguire's, Curran's position is still susceptible to this criticism since determining when the dying process begins is difficult now that we can put off some forms of dying by means of artificial life supports. Also, dying is more than just a physiological breakdown of organs and systems. Dying involves the total condition of the person. This includes all those conditions under which a person is willing to put oneself while the body breaks down. Intervening in a person's death negates the continuing trustworthiness of the dying person's life and the caring community's relationship to the dying. McCormick comes closest to protecting and promoting the trustworthiness of the dying and the caring community by holding fast to the prohibition against euthanasia as a practical absolute. His position can be effectively expanded by the vision of care and community which Stanley Hauerwas proposes.

The thought-pattern of proportionate reason upon which the mixed consequentialist position rests, however, has been subject to criticisms which could also weaken its approach to euthanasia.[50] One criticism is whether the basic value of life can be weighed against any other values (like dignity and freedom) as Maguire and Curran so weigh them. Germain Grisez, for example, claims that the essential weakness of this method lies in the comparative evaluation of values which it makes. That is to say, Grisez finds this method wrongly regarding as commensurable the benefits and harms which are really not on the same plane. For example, he maintains that the value of physical life cannot be weighed equally against the value of freedom, nor can meaningful life be weighed against a life with physical disability. Grisez claims that in every choice, some aspects of benefits and harm cannot be measured against one another or by any available common standards.[51] Such comparing and weighing of values remains a serious problem for ethical theory, even though we continue to compare unequal values all the time in our daily lives.

Another criticism focuses on the importance given to consequences in this approach. While proportionalism does include consequences, it also includes much more when it considers the action as a whole. Thus, the way of naming this position is often given as "moderate" or "mixed" consequentialism. The proportionate reason thought-pattern strives to avoid a one-sided consequentialism by trying to consider human nature and actions adequately. This means all aspects of an action must be considered, not just the consequences. McCormick's approach to euthanasia fulfills this better than the other two positions.

Another critical concern is whether this approach is too individualistic. Maguire's weighing of values and Curran's "dying process" may be open to this criticism since the role of the community to discern and maintain moral values and principles does not figure prominently in their analysis. McCormick, however, clearly wants to avoid individualism and protect the role of the community by calling for an examination of cultural values and attitudes in assessing a judgment of proportionality.

These concerns or reservations about this thought-pattern are worth raising. They show this approach is not complete in all respects. Cardinal Ratzinger, in fact, objects to any exclusive use of proportionalism as a method of moral judgment.[52] Yet this approach does deserve the attention of further development and evaluation as a method of moral judgment and as a way of addressing the issue of euthanasia.

Deontological Positions

The deontological positions include a variety of forms within a spectrum of possibilities. Only five will be considered. For the most part, the fundamental conviction of the deontological positions is that human life is a basic, but not an absolute good. These positions assume a moral posture that respects life and takes no direct action against it. However, this position does not oblige anyone to prolong life in every circumstance. Paul Ramsey, while following a deontological method, allows for a small "exception" to this obligation. His ethics would prohibit the direct intervention to bring about death only until the patient has progressed to the point of being beyond the reach of care and comfort. At this point Ramsey sees no moral difference between directly intervening to cause death and allowing the patient to die. This is what sets Ramsey apart from the deontological positions of the Vatican *Declaration on Euthanasia,* Grisez, Boyle, May, and Dyck with whom he agrees in most other ways. Finally, the extreme deontologism of vitalism regards human life as an absolute value that is inviolably sacred. Its moral posture is to protect life and do everything possible to prolong it.

Paul Ramsey

Princeton's Paul Ramsey has earned well-deserved respect among theologians over the years. He is often contrasted with Joseph Fletcher because of his consistent rule-oriented approach to ethics and his long-standing battle against ethical relativism. He can always be counted on for a thorough examination of all morally relevant issues related to specific moral problems. His treatment of euthanasia is no exception. His most thorough treatment of euthanasia is in his most comprehensive book on medical ethics, *The Patient as Person* (1970).[53]

Underlying Ramsey's approach to euthanasia is his conception of Christian ethics as an ethics of covenantal loyalty. "Fidelity to covenant" is the interpretive principle he uses to define the moral limits of medicine's duty to heal and to save life. The conscious acceptance of covenantal responsibilities is the inner meaning of all our relationships. The fundamental moral imperative of these relationships is to be faithful. With a view to this end, Ramsey's medical ethics aims

> to explore the meaning of *care,* to find the actions and abstentions that come from adherence to *covenant,* to ask the meaning of the *sanctity* of life, to articulate the requirements of steadfast *faithfulness* to a fellow man.[54]

His method keeps before us covenantally derived values which a Christian approach to medical-ethical questions must take into account, such as the sovereignty of God, the primacy of love, and God's covenantal love as the standard to which we are responsible as images of God.

Ramsey's stance toward euthanasia is clear and straightforward: euthanasia is immoral. He rejects all efforts to qualify euthanasia, since "euthanasia" for him is always choosing death as an end, pure and simple. For Ramsey the alternatives are either "euthanasia" or "dying well enough." This means that we can speak either of the immorality of euthanasia or of the morality of dying well enough. For this reason, he considers "euthanasia" to be an inappropriate term to describe efforts which cease to prolong life. He does this on the basis of accepting the moral distinction between commission and omission. He regards commissions, or hastening death, to be contrary to the faithfulness claims of covenant since commissions abandon care, a requirement of faithfulness. He regards omissions, on the other hand, to be within the canons of loyalty since omissions allow the patient to die from causes against which it is no longer reasonable to fight while the covenantal partners accompany the dying person with care.

Ramsey grounds the immorality of choosing death as an end on some fundamental religious convictions. One is that religious faith looks on life as a gift. To choose death, for Ramsey, would be "to throw the gift back in the face of the giver."[55] Moreover, religious faith affirms life as a trust of which we are stewards, not owners. To choose death is to abandon our trusteeship and deny that God is trustworthy. As trustees we do not lay claims to dominion or co-dominion over human life. Ramsey's ultimate religious warrant for prohibiting euthanasia is that it is incompatible with the demand of covenantal fidelity and its imperative never to abandon care. Ramsey holds up God's steadfast covenantal love for us as the standard for our fidelity to one another. Therefore,

> if we seriously mean to align our wills with God's care here and now for [the dying], there can never be any reason to hasten them from the here and now in which they still claim a faithful presence from us.[56]

To abandon care and to hasten the dying patient to death would be contrary to charity and fidelity.

After establishing the immorality of euthanasia, Ramsey is able to explore the moral limits of caring for the dying. His ethics of caring for the dying opposes two extremes: the vitalist extreme which says we must use all available means to preserve life, and the euthanasia extreme which justifies direct killing. This ethics, Ramsey believes, holds in the case of children no less than in that of adults.[57]

His ethics of only caring for the dying emerges out of his accepting a moral difference between omission and commission and the distinction between ordinary and extraordinary means of treatment. On the basis of these distinctions Ramsey can define the moral limits of the duty to save life. The distinctions recognize a difference between our obligations to the living and our obligations to the dying. When the patient is overcome by dying, we are not obligated to do all we can to keep the patient alive. Appropriate treatment for one overtaken by dying is care and comfort. Faithfulness-claims in such a situation exclude efforts to hasten death, but do not exclude administering death-hastening pain killers to relieve suffering. In fact, Ramsey interprets such acts as the positive meaning of acts of omission.

> Indeed, it is not quite right to say that we only care for the dying by an omission, by "doing nothing" directly or indirectly. Instead, we cease doing what was once called for and begin to do precisely what is called for now. We attend and company with him in this, his very own dying, rendering it as comfortable and dignified as possible.[58]

The covenantal relationship between the patient and the health-care providers does not include continuing useless efforts to cure, but it does include efforts to care. Acts of caring are deeds done for the dying to manifest to them that they are not forgotten or abandoned.

While insisting that the norm of only caring for the dying requires a moral difference between omission and commission, Ramsey recognizes that a patient may progress to the point of being beyond the reach of being given care and comfort and receiving it. In such an instance the distinction between omission and commission vanishes. This is what sets Ramsey apart from the other deontological positions of the *Vatican Declaration on Euthanasia*, Grisez, Boyle, May and Dyck with whom he agrees in most other ways.

If there is a point at which omission and commission become morally equivalent, one may then ask, "Is it morally permissible directly to terminate life that is beyond the reach of human caring?" Ramsey suggests that it is. He gives two examples of instances where this may be relevant for medical practice.

One case involves patients in irreversible coma whose lives are maintained for many years. The other involves patients undergoing deep and prolonged pain which cannot be relieved, such as bone cancer patients or infants suffering Lesch-Nyhan syndrome, a genetic illness for which there is no cure.[59] In both instances, Ramsey maintains, the judgment that a patient is in such a condition is proper to physicians, not moralists. And the reason for directly causing death in each instance is the same—namely, such patients would be beyond the reach of care and keeping company with them.

On the basis of this conclusion, Ramsey qualifies his rule of only caring for the dying by adding "exception clauses" to cover cases like those which he foresees as possible exceptions:

> 1. Never abandon care of the dying when they are irretrievably inaccessible to human care; never hasten the dying process except when it is *entirely indifferent* to the patient whether his dying is accomplished by an intravenous bubble of air or by the withdrawal of useless ordinary natural remedies, such as nourishment.

> 2. Always keep officious treatments away from the dying in order to draw close to them in companying with them and caring for them; never, therefore, take positive action to usher them out of our presence or to hasten their departure from the human community, *unless* there is a kind of prolonged dying in which it is medically impossible to keep severe pain at bay.[60]

In allowing for these exceptions, Ramsey does not fear a weakening of the general rule and practice of medicine to protect life as long as these exceptions stay within their limits as exceptions to the imperative to keep covenant with the dying.[61]

Ramsey's strict deontological position holds firm, then, to the protection of human life and advocates compassionate care, companying, and comfort of the dying. However, he is open to an exception to the prohibition of the direct termination of life in the limited exceptions of patients who might progress beyond the reach of care and comfort. With these exceptions carefully limited, he does not fear any abrogation of the principles prohibiting euthanasia.

Vatican Declaration on Euthanasia

On June 26, 1980 the Sacred Congregation for the Doctrine of the Faith issued its *Declaration on Euthanasia*.[62] This document is a brief but broad statement responding sensitively to the ethical issues surrounding the final stages of life. In developing its position, the document considers ethically relevant both Christian religious convictions as well as the accumulated wisdom of the human experience of suffering, sickness, dying and death. The purpose of the Declaration is to respond to bishops' questions about euthanasia and to offer them "elements for reflection" which they can present to the faithful and to civil authorities with regard to this matter.

This Declaration represents the official moral position on euthanasia of the Roman Catholic magisterium (the teaching authority of the Catholic hierarchy). Even though this is not an infallible teaching, it is still normative for the Catholic community. As "normative," this moral position deserves the presumption of truth on the part of the faithful. In the formation of their consciences on matters of caring for the dying, the faithful ought carefully to attend to this teaching. To say this, however, is not to say that this teaching is the exclusive basis of one's conscientious judgment. Nor does it say that no one may ever disagree with certain aspects of this teaching. For this teaching to be "normative" and for the faithful "to attend" to it means that this teaching deserves the respect, not of unquestioning or uncritical obedience, but of an attitude of docility which takes a critically alert, thoughtful and respectful approach to its interpretation and use.

The document has four main parts plus an introduction and conclusion. Part I lays out the fundamental conviction about the value of life and the basic norms which are derived from it. Life is the necessary source of every human activity. The Declaration recognizes that most people appreciate life as "something sacred." But for believers, life ought to be something more—

namely, "a gift of God's love, which they are called upon to preserve and make fruitful."

On this basis, the Declaration sets forth a series of three norms. The first is the universal prohibition against any attempts on the life of an innocent person. The second states the universal duty to live one's life in accord with God's plan that human life be fruitful and find its full perfection in eternal life. The third norm prohibits suicide on the grounds that suicide rejects God's sovereignty and plan, refuses to love self, denies the natural instinct to live, and avoids the duties of justice and charity. However, suicide is not to be confused with death which occurs as an act of self-sacrifice for love of others and the glory of God.

Part II of the Declaration expresses its understanding and subsequent prohibition of euthanasia. Its understanding fits the popular one of "mercy killing."

> By euthanasia is understood an action or an omission which of itself or by intention causes death, in order that all suffering may in this way be eliminated.

The terms of reference for euthanasia are "intention" and "methods." This understanding encompasses both the direct intervention that kills a person as well as the omission of planned inaction that intends to cause another to die. On this basis, euthanasia is forbidden for anyone along the continuum of life (from embryo to elderly) and in any condition of life (from one suffering from an uncurable disease to one who is clearly dying). No one is permitted to ask for euthanasia for oneself or another, consent to it, recommend it or permit it. In this light, the Declaration advises that the pleas of gravely ill persons for euthanasia are better interpreted as pleas not only for medical care, but also for human and supernatural support and comfort.

Part III offers elements for reflection on suffering. While recognizing that the fear and anguish of the prospect of death may be eased for some people who approach death by living through old age or a prolonged illness, the Declaration recognizes that suffering may so exceed its biological and psychological usefulness that it can cause the desire to remove it in any way and at whatever price. In some cases, a Christian evaluation of suffering which sees it as a participation in the redemptive suffering of Christ may lead some patients to limit their dosage of pain killing drugs in order to associate in a conscious way with the sufferings of Christ. However, the Declaration does not impose this heroic way of acting as a general rule. It acknowledges that most people will want to use analgesics and may do so even though these drugs will reduce consciousness and shorten life. Recalling the teaching of Pius XII in response to a question about whether or not narcotics can be used which will relieve pain but shorten life, the Declaration quotes Pius XII, saying, "If no other means exist, and if, in the given circumstances, this does not prevent the carrying out of other religious and moral duties: Yes." The Declaration goes on to explain that in such a case, death is not the direct object of intention. Pain relief is.

In Part IV the Declaration turns to the means that must be used to preserve life. It makes two points. The first pertains to who decides how the ill will live while dying. The second pertains to the principles in light of which the decision about remedies ought to be made. On the matter of who decides, the priority is given to the sick person. After first recognizing that complex situations can cause doubts about the way to apply principles, the Declaration continues,

> In the final analysis, it pertains to the conscience either of the sick person, or of those qualified to speak in the sick person's name, or of the doctors to decide in the light of moral obligations and of the various aspects of the case.

When turning to principles, the Declaration adverts to the standard terminology of "ordinary" and "extraordinary" means, but recognizes that these terms lack clarity. It cites with approval an alternative distinction between "proportionate" and "disproportionate" means. The proper judgment as to what means to use is the matter of balancing the type of means (considering its degree of complexity or risk, its cost and possibilities of use) and the result that can be expected (taking into consideration the state of the sick person and his or her physical and moral resources).

Proportionalism is the document's basic approach to applying the traditional principle of ordinary/extraordinary means when solving dilemmas affecting the duration of life. This means that it advocates the weighing of relative values (such as risk, cost, burden to patient and benefit) and recognizes that some means are disproportionate to the result sought. This proportionalism is clarified by considering some specific cases.

While first requiring the patient's consent, the document gives ethical approval to the use of risky and experimental techniques when alternative remedies are not available. It also permits abandoning such techniques when the results fall short of expectations, but again insists on the patient's consent, consideration of the reasonable wishes of the patient's family, and the advice of the doctors. The document also maintains that "it is permissible to make do with the normal means that medicine can offer." No one can be obliged to use a technique which is risky or burdensome. Such refusal is not suicide as long as the refusal of treatment is

> considered as an acceptance of the human condition, or a wish to avoid the application of a medical procedure disproportionate to the results that can be expected, or a desire not to impose excessive expense on the family or the community.

A refusal of treatment with the intention to end one's life would be considered suicide. This is always morally prohibited. Finally, when death is imminent, one may in good conscience

> refuse forms of treatment that would only secure a precarious and burdensome prolongation of life, so long as the normal care due the sick person in similar cases is not interrupted.

The Declaration concludes with two reflections. The one pertains to the believer's attitude toward death—death is unavoidable and we should be ready to accept it with full responsibility as the end of our earthly existence and as the opening to immortal life. The second pertains to those in the health care professions—while technical skills are certainly needed in caring for the sick and dying, "kindness and heartfelt charity" are even more so.

Avoiding denunciations and authoritarian language, the Declaration recognizes the complexity of issues surrounding the ending of life as well as the uniqueness of individual circumstances. It appreciates traditional wisdom in the Catholic tradition of medical ethics while at the same time recognizing the many obstacles to applying this wisdom in contemporary situations of health care. It not only is sensitive to the complexity of situations which cause doubts about the way principles should be applied, but it is also flexible in the way it states some principles. For example, the Declaration has accepted the wisdom underlying the principle of ordinary and extraordinary means, but allows a reformulation of this principle in terms of proportionate/disproportionate means in order to express this wisdom with greater clarity. However, it avoids strict utilitarianism, or situationalism, by positing certain general principles which set limits on what is morally acceptable. For example, the Declaration explicitly states that acts of mercy killing remain a grave moral evil even though moral culpability might be diminished by excusing causes:

> It may happen that, by reason of prolonged and barely tolerable pain, for deeply personal or other reasons, people may be led to believe that they can legitimately ask for death or obtain it for others. Although in these cases the guilt of the individual may be reduced or completely absent, nevertheless, the error of judgment into which the conscience falls, perhaps in good faith, does not change the nature of this act of killing, which will always be in itself something to be rejected.

In these ways the Vatican *Declaration on Euthanasia* is both respectful of basic values and principles of traditional Catholic medical ethics while being critical and flexible with regard to the particular application of them.

Germain Grisez, Joseph M. Boyle, Jr. and William E. May

Catholic philosophers Germain Grisez (Mount Saint Mary's College and Seminary, Emmitsburg, Maryland), Joseph M.

Boyle, Jr. (Center for Thomistic Studies, University of Houston) and moral theologian William E. May (Catholic University of America) will be considered together as representatives of another deontological position since they follow the same thought-pattern in their approach to euthanasia. Grisez and Boyle have collaborated on a substantial book *Life and Death with Liberty and Justice* (1979),[63] which is a significant contribution to the euthanasia debate. This book is essentially a treatment of the jurisprudential questions related to euthanasia, though it has two substantial chapters on the ethics of euthanasia. May follows the same thought-pattern as Grisez and Boyle in his major book on medical ethics, *Human Existence, Medicine and Ethics* (1977).[64]

These men construct their position against euthanasia by challenging two basic assumptions of a pro-euthanasia position. One is the anthropological assumption that human life is an instrumental good necessary for personal fulfillment. The other is the methodological assumption that consequences alone determine the rightness or wrongness of human acts. Grisez, Boyle and May argue that human, bodily life is a constitutive good, intrinsic to human persons and contributes directly to human fulfillment. Methodologically they argue against consequentialism in favor of a deontological form of moral reasoning based on incommensurate goods of human persons and an emphasis on the attitude (Grisez and Boyle), or intention (May), of the person toward these goods.

Grisez, Boyle and May find an unsupportable dualism in the anthropology implicit in pro-euthanasia positions. This dualism maintains a sharp distinction between bodily life and personal life. It regards the personal component as the truly valuable component and renders the bodily component a merely instrumental good providing the necessary material condition for the fulfillment of the personal. This makes the bodily component the means to the end of personal activity. The personal component is what enables the human individual to control affairs through rational choice. It is the distinctively human component which is not yet present in the unborn or newly born and which is lost in the irreversibly comatose. The absence of this personal component is what makes one a candidate for euthanasia.

Against this dualism, the anthropology of Grisez, Boyle and May regards the human being as one. According to them, bodily life participates in the integrity of the person as a substantive good of human life, and human life is the life of a personal being. While not an absolute good (since only God is that), bodily life is a good deserving reverence and respect. Their position can be summarized this way:

> Life is not only a condition which is necessary if a person is to achieve higher values. It is an intrinsic aspect of human flourishing; it directly contributes to the full dignity of the human person. Hence, although human life is not an absolute, superior to all other personal goods, neither is it merely instrumental.[65]

This anthropology of bodily and personal integrity is foundational to their ethical method which begins with the premise that there are certain basic human goods constitutive of human well-being and which are realized, to a greater or lesser degree, by actions in which the whole person participates. The fundamental human goods which are inherently worthwhile, give meaning to one's life, and serve as motives for human action are these: play and recreation, knowledge of truth and appreciation of beauty, life and health, friendship and self-integration.[66] This is not meant to be an exhaustive list, nor are these goods presented in a hierarchical order, since these goods cannot be measured one against another to establish a hierarchy. These basic human goods provide motives for moral action and are the source of the moral obligation to promote human well-being.

While these basic human goods clarify what is possible in moral choice, they do not determine by themselves morally good or evil choices. What determines this? Moral goodness and moral evil depend on the attitude, or intention, the person takes toward these basic goods. A right moral attitude, or intention, is to be open to all the basic goods, even those not immediately chosen or realized.

> The basic requirement of morality is that one choose and act for some human goods, while at the same time one maintain

one's appreciation, openness, and respect for the goods one is
not *now* acting for.[67]

This means that each basic good must be allowed to exercise its
influence on human well-being even when we are not pursuing
one or some of them. Grisez and Boyle identify four modes of
moral obligation by which we remain open to these basic goods
and show respect for them: we take them into account in our conduct; we prefer ways to enhance these goods rather than inhibit
them; we make an effort to support these values when their real-
ization in another person is endangered; we never turn directly
against any one of them.[68] Our minimal obligation is this last
one—that we never act directly against a basic good. On this
basis, Grisez and Boyle conclude that certain types of choices are
absolutely prohibited. These are any choices which are directed
against one of the basic goods.[69]

On this basis Grisez, Boyle and May absolutely prohibit
euthanasia because it intends to realize some good (such as freedom or dignity) by directly turning against one or more basic
goods (life or health). Euthanasia wrongly assumes that the
choice for death over life can be morally right because it serves
the higher goods of freedom, integrity or dignity. But according
to the thought pattern of Grisez, Boyle and May, the basic goods
cannot be so compared and balanced off each other. May concludes in his critique of an ethics of euthanasia:

> A sound moral policy, reflecting a heart that is open to all that
> is good and worthwhile, requires us to love and respect all the
> real goods of human beings, of human persons. These goods
> are not comparable and cannot be weighed one against
> another.[70]

Yet this position does not yield a vitalistic ethics making life
itself the highest good. If clinging to human life in a vitalistic way
requires us to turn against other basic goods, like freedom, integrity or dignity, then such actions of preserving life would also be
immoral. Although death is not a good worthy of human choice,
it is not an evil to be prevented at all cost. Grisez, Boyle and May

recognize the moral significance of the distinction between commission and omission and ordinary and extraordinary means of treatment. These give the dying patient the moral right to refuse any treatment that would only prolong the dying which itself is attacking the basic goods of freedom, dignity or integrity.

While killing (e.g., voluntary and non-voluntary euthanasia) is an action of directly turning against the basic good of life, not every death-dealing deed (e.g., refusing, withdrawing or withholding life-prolonging treatment) is an act of killing in the morally strict sense. The difference lies in acting directly against a basic good or acting in a way that directly interferes with realizing a basic good. Herein lies the moral significance of the distinction between commission and omission which, in turn, relies on the distinction between the direct and indirect intention. To allow the destruction or interference of a basic good to occur as an unavoidable side-effect of an effort to pursue a basic good is one thing. But it is quite another to act directly against a basic good or to interfere directly with realizing it. On these grounds, for example, directly taking human life is strictly prohibited. On the other hand, acts of omission are morally permissible because we do not set our wills (or directly intend to act) against the dying person's life by intending to terminate his or her life. Such acts of omission are not acts contrary to basic human goods because of the positive attitude or intention to embrace the basic goods.[71]

William E. May summarizes the heart of this deontological approach based on the fundamental moral requirement never to act directly against a basic good. His summary will serve as a fitting conclusion to this deontological position:

> . . . a human being cannot rightfully do a deed that is destructive of a human good such as life, unless in the doing of that deed the agent's intent and the thrust of his act are both targeted on the good achievable in and through that deed. In such instances the evil caused is an inevitable and inescapable element or partial aspect of the entire human deed, and the evil is an aspect that is not of necessity intended by the doer. Such deeds may be directly destructive of a human good in a *physical* way, but they are not directly destructive in the order of

human intentionality inasmuch as they are not intended in any proper sense but are rather foreseen and permitted. . . . I ought not to be willing to do a deed that will require, as an inevitable necessity, that I am willing to set myself in my will (biblically my "heart") against a real good of another human being, of another being of moral worth, that requires me to say of these goods here and now that they are non-goods, no longer worthy of my love and respect.[72]

Arthur J. Dyck

Harvard's Arthur J. Dyck has examined the underlying presuppositions of an ethic of euthanasia and has rejected them. He lists these presuppositions as the following:

(1) That an individual's life belongs to that individual to dispose of entirely as he or she wishes;
(2) That the dignity that attaches to personhood by reason of the freedom to make moral choices demands also the freedom to take one's own life;
(3) That there is such a thing as a life not worth living, whether by reason of distress, illness, physical or mental handicaps, or even sheer despair for whatever reason;
(4) That what is sacred or supreme in value is the "human dignity" that resides in man's own rational capacity to choose and control life and death.[73]

The ethical framework of Dyck's position is elaborated in his book, *On Human Care* (1977).[74] Because "euthanasia" has lost its meaning as a merely descriptive term for a happy and good death, Dyck finds it necessary to invent a new term—namely, "benemortasia." Both an ethic of euthanasia and an ethic of benemortasia value compassion and freedom, but they differ on the ways best to realize these values. Dyck's benemortasia challenges euthanasia through the notion of mercy as expressed in the Good Samaritan ideal. Whereas an ethic of euthanasia would deliberately induce death, an ethic of benemortasia retreats to "caring only" in the face of inevitable death and "seeks to reduce pain and suffering as much as possible but not to the point of directly inducing death."[75] The mercy expressed in benemortasia is a pledge not only not to kill but also to be the sort of person who provides care for those who need it. The care to patients who are nearing death is at least fourfold: "(1) relief of pain; (2) relief of suffering; (3) respect for patients' right to refuse treatment; and (4) administering of health care regardless of ability to pay."[76]

The ethical framework of benemortasia supports the values of human life by putting certain constraints on human freedom. One constraint comes in the priority Dyck gives to the principle of non-maleficence over the principal of beneficence. With this he stands in stark contrast to Marvin Kohl. The principle of non-maleficence upholds one of the traditional ethical priorities of medicine—namely, first of all, do no harm. Kohl does not include this obligation in his definition of kindness. In Dyck's view, if harm is ever inflicted, it can be justified only on the grounds that life and health are better served by it in the long run, if not in the short run.[77]

Dyck also argues on the basis of the prohibition against killing found in the Judeo-Christian Decalogue-covenant.[78] To say that taking a human life is wrong does not mean that an act of killing or subjecting someone to the risk of death may never be justified. But if such acts are to be justified, they will be so for reasons that do not undermine the presumption that life is precious and that everyone has a right to life. Dyck finds such justifying reasons to end life present in a case of trying to prevent a murder or in a case of an indirect abortion to save a woman's life. In either instance, the taking of human life is a tragic by-product of an effort to protect and save life.[79]

Another Judeo-Christian restraint on freedom is the limited knowledge humans have of good and evil and the ultimate destiny of persons.

> Only God could have such knowledge. Trying to decide who shall live and who shall die is "playing god." It is tragic to "play god" because one does it with such limited and uncertain knowledge of what is good and evil.[80]

This constraint on freedom liberates the dying person to accept his or her dying and secures the right of the patient to choose the circumstances under which the terminal illness will take its course. The dying patient retains the right to accept or refuse medical treatment when no cure is available.

In light of these constraints on freedom, Dyck's argument leans heavily on two distinctions that have been traditional in Catholic circles: the distinction between allowing to die and causing death, and that between the direct and indirect intentions of our actions. Unlike Ramsey, he gives no indication of any limits to the usefulness of these distinctions. For example, the case of the irreversibly comatose poses a special challenge. Dyck recognizes that in such tragic circumstances, no decision is totally satisfactory from a moral point of view. He defends, however, the standpoint of benemortasia:

> From the standpoint of our ethic of benemortasia, there is a strong presumption to continue to support the comatose and the severely brain damaged until there is no reasonable hope of improving or reversing their condition. And when such a point is reached despite every effort, it may be kind to withdraw from massive, sustained efforts—involving a respirator, for example—in the face of the next serious bout of illness where such episodes are expected to continue and be frequent until fatal.[81]

In other words, in the ethics of benemortasia, one is free to give one's life over to death by refusing non-curative care that prolongs dying, but one is not free to take one's own life by directly inducing death. Deliberate acts to end life, or suicide, cannot be justified since causing one's own death does violence to one's self and harms others. However, the dying person may choose to use a potent dose of a pain killing drug for the sake of relieving pain, even though it has the effect of shortening life. The difference is in the intention.[82]

Thus, in his ethics of benemortasia, Dyck argues for the following beliefs and values:

(1) that an individual person's life is not solely at the disposal of that person; every human life is part of the human community that bestows and protects the lives of its members;

the possibility of community itself depends upon constraints against taking life;

(2) that the dignity that attaches to personhood by reason of the freedom to make moral choices includes the freedom of dying people to refuse noncurative, life-prolonging interventions when one is dying, but does not extend to taking one's life or causing death for someone who is dying;

(3) that every life has some worth; there is no such thing as a life not worth living;

(4) that the supreme value is goodness itself to which the dying and those who care for the dying are responsible. Religiously expressed the supreme value is God. Less than perfectly good beings, human beings, require constraints upon their decisions regarding those who are dying. No human being or human community can presume to know who deserves to live or die.[83]

Vitalism

Vitalism is the most extreme form of a deontological position and the polar opposite of the positions considered under strict consequentialism. It represents the stance that regards human life as an absolute and inviolably sacred value. Its posture is to protect life and to do everything possible to prolong it. Even though no contemporary philosopher or theologian writing on euthanasia today defends this position in its pure form, its main lines and spirit need to be understood since it is often mistaken as the official Catholic position, and because it is the position against which other positions on euthanasia are stated or with which they are at least often contrasted.

Vitalism is often readily associated with Albert Schweitzer and his doctrine of *Ehrfurcht vor dem Leben* (Reverence for Life). Schweitzer's African experience of moving through an environment saturated with vitality evoked a deep reverence for all life and led to his avowal to avoid killing life as much as possible. He writes:

There slowly grew up in me an unshakeable conviction that we have no right to inflict suffering and death on another living creature unless there is some unavoidable necessity for it, and that we ought all of us to feel what a horrible thing it is to cause suffering and death out of mere thoughtlessness.[84]

For Schweitzer "reverence for life" was the fundamental basis of ethics. Its master conviction was that "the good consists in the preservation, enhancement, and exaltation of life and that the destruction, injury, and retardation of life is evil."[85] However, caricatures of this doctrine lead to believing that life in any form can never be taken under any conditions. This is not Schweitzer's position. He recognizes that, even while respecting life, the taking of life is at times an unavoidable necessity done with great regret. As he says:

> If he holds to the ethic of reverence of life, he injures or destroys life only under a necessity which cannot be escaped. Never does such a man annihilate living forms from thoughtlessness. Insofar as he is a free being, he seeks out every opportunity of partaking of the blessedness of advancing and assisting life and of protecting it from misery and destruction.[86]

A more recent advocate of a pro-vitalist position is Dr. David Karnofsky, a tumor research scientist of the Sloan-Kettering Institute of New York. In the 1961 meeting of the American Cancer Society, Dr. Karnofsky defended a pro-vitalist position by rejecting any advice to withhold aggressive treatment and arguing for prolonging life in the hope that during a temporary reprieve a more effective treatment might be found. He gives an example of what he means by aggressive care. He tells of a patient with cancer of the large bowel. A colostomy was performed to relieve an intestinal blockage. X-ray treatment relieved cancer recurring in a nearby area. Radioactive phosphorus relieved the abdominal cavity filling with fluid. Bronchopneumonia was cured by an antibiotic. X-rays were again used to halt the spread of cancer to the liver. With all this, the patient lived for ten months. Without any of these measures, the patient would have died within days or weeks. Dr. Karnofsky asked, "When should the physician stop treating this patient?" He answers, "I believe he must carry on until the issue is taken out of his hands."[87]

Dr. Marshall Brummer, a pulmonary specialist, shares Dr. Karnofsky's convictions about vitalism. In 1981, the President's Commission asked him, "Is it the duty of the physician to do everything for that patient until that patient is called to his or her reward?" He answered, "Yes." He further commented that he did not regard permanent maintenance on a respirator to be an heroic measure.[88]

Such vitalist attitudes are also evident in a policy statement of the Worcester Hahnemann Hospital:

> "No one, patient, family or physician, may consent to, direct or initiate the removal or withdrawal of care or treatment which may be considered in any way to be life sustaining to any patient, except as provided below." The "provision below" was that the patient be dead according to the so-called Harvard Criteria of Death and be declared so by the attending physician.[89]

Similarly, superintendent William E. Jones of the Belchertown State School in Massachusetts instructed all health care personnel caring for Belchertown patients that "the Administration of this facility holds the preservation of life to be ultimate and expects that all known techniques to prolong the life of the client be utilized unless countermanded by Court decree."[90]

The vitalistic outlook, then, holds to biological survival as a first-order value. While it is not a position defended by philosophers or theologians participating in the discussion on euthanasia, vitalism is still held by some health-care professionals. This outlook leads to an unqualified defense of human life in every form and condition and to the unconditional preservation of physical life. All other considerations, such as personality, personal integrity and dignity, freedom and self-possession, take a secondary place to sustaining physical life. This position would maintain that God alone has absolute dominion over life and death. Our obligation is to sustain human life without reservation.

Deontological Positions: An Assessment

These deontological positions show one of the greatest strengths of this approach. It clearly emphasizes the moral necessity of protecting even weakened life. By upholding the principle prohibiting killing as a basic, universal principle, the deontological approach clearly supports the social fabric of the human community. It upholds the worth of human life in every condition and supports the trustworthiness of all human relationships. By respecting the distinction between omission and commission, it recognizes the limit of human efforts to cure and transforms that obligation into one of caring for those who cannot be cured.

The deontological extreme of vitalism, however, so absolutizes physical life that no amount of suffering or physical disability could ever justify withholding or withdrawing treatment. Vitalism interprets the sick and dying person too narrowly. It reduces the dying to a physiological organism. It fails to account for the personal dimensions of being human which entail certain beliefs, values, aspirations and perspectives on the meaning of life and death. It also fails to consider that part of caring for the dying is not to prolong death needlessly with every available means and at any cost.

Paul Ramsey's "exceptions" to the principle forbidding interventions to take life have some difficulties. He does not indicate whether the person who is beyond care must necessarily be dying, or just be deeply unconscious but very much alive otherwise. By drawing the line for the limits of the principle against killing at the point of the person no longer being able to experience care, Ramsey seems to be suggesting a quality of life criterion. Anyone "inaccessible to care," meaning anyone unable to experience care, would seem to have such a low quality of life that such a life is not worth living. Is this what Ramsey means? Furthermore, his exceptions require reliable evidence to verify that a person is unable to experience care. Without reliable criteria to make this judgment, the exceptions may be ill-founded and we would end up killing those who are not able to communicate their wishes to us, and who may not want to be killed if they could only let us know.

A point of criticism that could be leveled at the deontological method as a whole is one which reaches to the finer points of moral argument and ethical theory. The deontological argument against euthanasia relies on the moral difference between direct and indirect intention so that no one may ever act directly against the basic good of life. Direct killing is always forbidden as morally evil, though indirect killing may be permitted. The key to this argument is our ability to describe moral objectivity adequately. A significant feature of this description is the distinction between moral and non-moral evil. The deontological argument does not uphold this distinction which is fundamental to the arguments of mixed consequentialist positions.

Bruno Schüller has argued that the direct/indirect distinction has moral relevance only where a moral evil is the intended consequence. We have no morally significant difference between direct and indirect intentions where non-moral evils are concerned.[91] Schüller, along with Richard McCormick and others, would argue that whether an action is morally evil or not depends on the total significance of the action. For only when we have grasped the total significance of the action do we have the true moral object which can be evaluated as morally evil or not. Direct and indirect provide a descriptive difference of what is being sought, by what means, and in what circumstances. The combination of these reveals the significance of an action. Not until we know the significance of the action as a whole are we able to tell whether our manner of pursuing them is destructive of them or not. Euthanasia ought to be prevented, not because it is direct killing, but because when killing for mercy is taken as a whole the non-moral evil outweighs the good. We cannot make this judgment, however, until we understand the relationship of all aspects of the action, not just whether the killing was directly or indirectly intended.

While the conclusions of the deontological position and the mixed consequentialist positions can be and are often the same, the attitude toward the principle prohibiting killing and what counts as evidence in making a moral judgment will often differ. However, the deontological position ought to be taken seriously as a viable way to approach the discussion of euthanasia. It regards life as a basic value and the principle forbidding killing as a basic principle. In these ways it provides an approach which will protect and enhance the character of the dying and the caring community surrounding the dying. The finer points of ethical theory which still need further discussion do not hinder the larger contribution this approach can make to the character of the caring community.

Conclusion

What can we make of the unity and diversity in this survey of positions? The conclusions reached by the representatives of each position are the least interesting part of this survey. A more interesting part has to do with the relationship of shared principles and methods to the prudential judgments each representative makes. For example, on the one hand, McCormick, Dyck, Grisez, Boyle and May use different methods but come to virtually the same conclusion. (I say "virtually" the same because there is a slight difference.) For Grisez, Boyle and May, directly turning against a basic good is intrinsically morally evil. Anything intrinsically morally evil cannot be open to any exceptions under any circumstances. For McCormick, however, directly turning against a basic good is a premoral evil needing justification by a proportionate reason. McCormick's conclusion that the direct termination of life is "virtually exceptionless" is a careful qualification open to the possibility of an exception, even though remote.

If we compare Maguire and Fletcher, we find another case of two different methods leading to similar conclusions. On the other hand, McCormick, Maguire and Curran use similar methods but come to somewhat different conclusions about the moral rightness of the direct termination of life. From this we can learn that endorsing the same principles and thought-patterns of moral reasoning does not solve cases or give answers. Ultimately principles and thought-patterns inform prudence. They do not replace it. Formulated principles and a thought-pattern like proportionalism, for example, can only prepare one intellectually and psychologically for a decision. They do not make the decision for us. So much for the limitation of our principles and methods.

Another interesting part of the euthanasia discussion is both in the philosophical and theological presuppositions each uses to conceive the relevant issues pertaining to euthanasia, and in the ethical method each uses to resolve the problems identified as crucial. This survey shows that much of the controversy over euthanasia can be explained as a matter of conflicting philosophical and theological presuppositions and ethical methods. For example, while each might hold to the sanctity or dignity of life as a primordial value, not everyone expresses the reverence due that life in the same way or to the same degree. So to hold to common values in the euthanasia discussion does not necessarily lead to the same moral policy.

Yet amidst the diversity on the continuum, we find that most agree on the important moral issues and principles at stake in the discussion. Such unity encourages further collaboration on these issues and is an optimistic sign for developing a social consensus on them. Another optimistic sign coming out of this survey is to see that the convergence of philosophical and religious ethics is possible. Philosophers and theologians approaching moral issues from quite different perspectives can work together. The diversity of philosophical and theological representatives in this survey shows that these two traditions are compatible in many respects and may be able to work together toward consensus.

4
Caring for the Dying

Now that we have considered the underlying issues of the euthanasia discussion and some of the alternative positions, we can turn to some ethical considerations of terminal care which this discussion of euthanasia raises: (1) Who should decide whether life-prolonging treatments should be used? (2) Should the dying person be told the truth about his or her condition? (3) What is hospice and how does it fit within the larger discussion of euthanasia?

Who Decides?

The central issue of the question "Who decides?" is brought into focus by the question which is the title of Brian Clark's play originally written for British television but which has since become successful on stage and screen, *Whose Life Is It Anyway?* The fundamental issue is the locus of power and control in matters of health, life and death. In the clinical setting, the moral principles which direct health care personnel to do what benefits the patient often conflict with principles which enhance the patient's autonomy, or self-determination. For example, a common clinical practice is to allow a dying patient to die by withholding CPR when the patient suddenly needs it to revive. The policy of many hospitals is that resuscitation efforts will be made unless the attending physician writes an order not to resuscitate (also known as a "no code" order). The ethical question is: Who should make the "no code" decision? Does the doctor know best? Or does the patient, the patient's family, a hospital committee, the court? Whose life is it anyway?

The consensus of the moral literature affirms that the primary decision-maker in life-prolonging decisions is the person whose life is in question. The principles of respect for persons and self-determination establish a presumption in favor of the patient's choices and limit the extent of medical intervention intended to benefit the patient. The medical-moral tradition assumes the right of the patient with proper mental capacity to use or refuse life-prolonging treatment. Pius XII in his allocution "The Prolongation of Life" stated that the doctor has only those rights over the patient which the patient gives the doctor. Traditional authors, like Gerald Kelly,[1] as well as contemporary ones, like Robert Veatch,[2] affirm this. Within the framework of personal care, the doctor may have the special skills to know the natural history of the patient's condition with or without treatment. But the doctor can claim no special skill in answering the moral question of what ought to be done. While the patient needs to be informed by the input of medical judgments, the patient retains the priority in deciding what ought to be done in light of his or her vision of life. The hard question is whether the patient is competent, or has the mental capacity to make such a decision.

Assessing Competence or The Capacity To Choose

In answering "Who decides?" we need to distinguish between competent and incompetent patients. While the terms "competent" and "incompetent" are frequently used in reference to the capacity to choose for oneself in a medical situation, Jonsen, Siegler and Winslade, in their book *Clinical Ethics,* prefer to restrict the use of these terms to the legal status of the patient where these terms refer to the patient's ability to understand the nature and consequences of decisions. In the clinical situation, however, Jonsen and his colleagues prefer the terms "mental capacity" or "incapacity" to describe the patient's ability to understand the medical situation and make choices about it. They describe "incapacity" as developmental or pathological.

Developmental incapacity refers to the immature mental processes of infants, children or the developmentally disabled. Pathological incapacity arises from psychopathological conditions such as coma, dementia or psychosis.[3]

Considerable disagreement exists over criteria for determining capacity. The President's Commission, summarizing the direction of much of the literature on determining competence or the capacity to choose, requires to a greater or lesser degree:

> (1) possession of a set of values and goals; (2) the ability to communicate and to understand information; and (3) the ability to reason and to deliberate about one's choices.[4]

The first element requires a reasonably consistent framework for comparing options and evaluating outcomes in light of reasonably stable values and goals. The second includes the possession of various linguistic and conceptual skills to give and receive information. The third element involves the ability to compare the impact of alternative outcomes on personal values and life plans.

Assessing this capacity is not easy. The President's Commission recommends that the assessment must balance the competing values of a patient's well-being and self-determination by taking into account the potential consequences of the patient's decision. This means that a patient's simply expressing a preference about a treatment is not enough to demonstrate this capacity to choose. It also means that this capacity should not be based on the objective considerations of the content of the decision. While the patient may be exercising self-determination by expressing a preference, this preference may actually be contradictory to the patient's values and goals which self-determination is trying to uphold. Also, a decision that may be "objectively correct" may inadequately reflect what the patient wants for his or her own life.[5] From this the commission concludes:

> What is relevant is whether someone is in fact capable of making a particular decision as judged by the consistency between the person's choice and that individual's underlying values

and by the extent to which the choice promotes the individual's well-being as he or she sees it.[6]

The commission favors giving the presumption of capacity to the patient and accepting what the patient decides, unless the decision clearly does not promote the patient's well-being in conformity with his or her expressed preferences, values and goals. This avoids declaring a patient incapable of making a choice simply because the patient rejects conventional wisdom about health care, or shares a certain status, such as being mentally retarded, comatose, or a child.[7]

Refusal of Treatment

This approach to assessing capacity does not hold that the right to refuse treatment is absolute. James Childress and Paul Ramsey have addressed its limits. In his book *Who Should Decide?*[8] James Childress approaches the question from his analysis of paternalism in health care. He favors a form of "weak paternalism" which gives the presumption in favor of the patient's choices while still recognizing the possibility of overriding the patient's preference for a time in order to validate the mental capacity of the patient and the reasonableness of the choice. As he says,

> Although it is not morally permissible to kill patients or to let patients die for the sake of others, it is sometimes justifiable to keep them alive even against their wishes for the sake of others (e.g., a child's need for a mother). And "weak" paternalistic interferences with a patient's decisions are sometimes justified. They must, however, meet a heavy burden of proof.[9]

For Paul Ramsey, the distinction between dying and non-dying patients is the key to understanding the limitations he puts on the right to refuse treatment. "Who decides?" for Ramsey is relative to the medical indications for treatment. What is medically indicated differs for the dying and non-dying. Rather than speaking of the patient's right to refuse treatment, Ramsey encourages the patient to participate in the decisions affecting him or her. This includes the choice to refuse any further treatment which prolongs dying. However, in the case of the *non-dying* patient, ethical care calls for using medically indicated treatments to save life.

> There are medically indicated treatments (these used to be called "ordinary") that a competent conscience patient has no moral right to refuse, just as no one has a moral right deliberately to ruin his health.[10]

Ramsey accepts a patient's refusal of treatment only when the treatment merely prolongs dying. He does not accept the refusal of treatment which would prolong life. For Ramsey, then, the objective considerations of the patient's condition and what is medically indicated for such a condition prevail over the patient's wishes as determinants of what to do. The patient's right to refuse treatment is only a relative right. For Ramsey, it does not extend beyond the medical judgment of what ought to be done, since what is medically indicated is morally what ought to be done.[11]

Proxy Judgments

The truly hard cases of "Who decides?" involve those patients who cannot make decisions for themselves. Some have lost consciousness; others may be unable to communicate their desires; some are irrational or too confused to decide, while others are overwhelmed with fear. These are instances of patients who have lost their mental capacity to understand the medical situation and to make choices. Who decides for them? The Vatican *Declaration on Euthanasia* answers:

> In the final analysis, it pertains to the conscience either of the sick person, or of those qualified to speak in the sick person's name, or of the doctors to decide in the light of moral obligations and of the various aspects of the case.

In short, this *Declaration* acknowledges the validity of a proxy judgment, and it affirms that the task of making this judgment falls on those who presumably have the best knowledge of and concern for the patient.

That we must make proxy judgments is clear. But we are not clear on how best to do it. Two standards are being promoted to guide proxy judgments—the "substituted judgment" standard and the "best interests" standard. According to the "substituted judgment" standard, the proxy ought to choose what the patient would have chosen if he or she were capable. This standard attempts to extend patient autonomy and to serve the patient's own definition of well-being. According to the "best interests" standard, the proxy judges on the basis of what promotes the welfare of the hypothetical "reasonable person" in the position of the patient. This judgment does not refer to the patient's actual or supposed preference, but to what would "reasonably" promote the patient's well-being. This standard is necessary for patients who have never had the mental capacity to understand and choose (e.g., infants), or who, while once having this capacity, did not make their wishes known.

Substituted Judgment Standard

The President's Commission favors the substituted judgment standard for proxy judgments whenever possible, "since it promotes the underlying values of self-determination and well-being better than the best interest standard does."[12] The substituted judgment standard requires that the patient has once expressed his or her wishes for treatment when there is no hope of recovery. To the extent possible, proxy decisions following this standard ought to be consistent and compatible with what is known of the patient's values and preferences. Normally, the next of kin would be the best judge of this, though not necessarily or always. A patient could use various degrees of explicitness and formality in expressing his or her values and preferences. For example, the least explicit and least formal way would be to infer a patient's desires from the person's value history, including at least the person's biography, aspirations, life style and life plan. A more explicit but still informal way of expressing one's wishes is through general conversation with one's family and friends about death and treatment of the dying. The most explicit and formal expression of one's wishes would be through something like a "living will" document.

Living Wills

"Living wills" have been receiving some attention in the past decade, especially in light of cases like those of Karen Quinlan and Br. Fox, and legislation like the California Natural Death Act (1976), the first legal recognition of the living will. The appearance of living wills is a strong affirmation that patients should have substantial control over their medical care to the very end of life. The living will is a written statement drawn up while a person has the mental capacity to give directions for the sort of treatment he or she would prefer in the event he or she were diagnosed as terminally ill and should become unable to provide any further instruction.

The functions of living wills are multiple. The foremost function is to maximize patient autonomy, and therefore dignity. Living wills do this by giving the patient control over the end of his or her life should he or she become incapable of understanding the medical situation and making any further choices. Also, a living will relieves the dying patient of making hard choices at a time when he or she no longer has the strength to consider alternative forms of care. Living wills with legally binding force (e.g., California's Natural Death Act) as well as those without legally binding force (e.g., Catholic Hospital Association's "Christian Affirmation of Life") serve equally to assist the substituted judgment of proxy representation. But those which are legally binding also protect the physician, paramedics, and health care facilities from civil or criminal liability for withholding or withdrawing treatment when they act according to the provisions of the will.[13]

While the tradition of medical ethics justifies the living will in principle, its difficulties lie in its application. Living wills often use vague language like "extraordinary," "heroic," or "useless treatment," and "reasonable expectation of recovery." Interpreting exactly what a patient wants in a given medical condition is not easy. The terms of living wills need to be clarified by discussion with one's primary physician as well as with family members. In the absence of such clarification, the living will becomes one piece of evidence among other expressions of the patient's preference. These together with medical indicators contribute to the judgment of what ought to be done.[14]

Whether living-will statutes (natural death acts) are necessary and helpful remains an open question. Some, like many state Catholic Conferences as well as theologian Karen Labacqz and attorney Dennis Horan, think they create more problems than they solve, and in reality give nothing to persons they do not already possess under the law and within long-standing religious and moral traditions.[15] The President's Commission finds their greatest value to be in the impetus they provide for a discussion about life-sustaining treatment. But the commission also recognizes that this discussion can be obtained without making these documents binding by law.[16]

Initially, Richard McCormick collaborated with Andre Hellegers to oppose legislation of living wills in the wake of the California legislation. Their opposition stemmed not from what the legislation sought to achieve—namely, protecting the self-determination of the patient—but from what it might actually produce. For instance, the very fact that a law is needed to assure patients' rights implies that the locus of control is not first in the patient but in the doctor, and that the proxy exercise of rights does not first belong to the family or guardian. Thus, living-will legislation could undermine a patient's self-determination and proxy rights rather than defend them, by raising the entire question of who has control and proxy rights when no living will has been written.[17]

Four years of state supreme court decisions on the termination of life prompted a second look at living-will legislation. This time Richard McCormick collaborated with John Paris to reconsider opposing such legislation.[18] While still believing that patients may express their desires for treatment to physicians without the support of legislation, the judicial decisions of several state supreme courts, together with the belief of many physicians, attorneys and legislators that the patient's statement has no legitimacy without a statutory enactment, forced them to revise their opposition to living-will legislation. The decision in the Br. Fox case underscored the need. In that case, the court upheld that the right to refuse treatment belongs to the patient alone. Judge Meade held that the right of self-determination takes priority over the substituted judgment of the proxy. The judge permitted the removal of life support measures from Br. Fox only because he had indicated while still mentally capable that he would not consent to continuing life-supportive measures if he were ever in a situation like Karen Quinlan. The court acted on behalf of this already expressed wish, and not on behalf of Fr. Eichner's (the proxy's) request. The court's ruling insisted on "clear and convincing" evidence that the patient, when having the mental capacity to do so, had expressed his or her desire not to be treated when there was no hope of recovery. This led McCormick and Paris to conclude that the most reliable method of indicating one's desires is in a written statement. They were willing to withdraw their opposition to living-will legislation as long as subsequent legislation would recognize "the dignity and natural moral rights of the person," has "carefully drawn provisions to protect those without living wills," and "prohibits any form of active euthanasia."[19]

Durable Power of Attorney for Health Care

A simpler and more flexible legal document for making health care decisions on behalf of the incompetent patient is the Durable Power of Attorney for Health Care (DPAHC). "Powers of attorney" statutes are already familiar legal devices used primarily to settle small property interests. But the power of attorney becomes null and void when the person who authorized it becomes incapacitated. These statutes would become inoperative in health care just when we needed them most. For this reason, these statutes are of no use in health care for making decisions for the mentally incapable. "Durable" power of attorney statutes, however, do allow the person's authority to continue after he or she has lost the mental capacity to understand and choose. Nearly all the states now have made it possible to create "durable" power of attorney which can be used for health care decisions.

Living wills and DPAHC are similar in some respects, but differ in significant ways. Like the living will, the DPAHC is prepared in advance of the onset of serious illness and diminished capacity for decision-making. Also, like the living will, its purpose is to extend the expression of the patient's wishes for medical treatment into the future when the patient's actual expression of treatment preference will be impossible or difficult to obtain.

However, the DPAHC differs from the living will in some significant ways. Whereas living wills apply only in terminal illness when death is imminent, DPAHC applies in all situations in which the patient is unable to make his or her decisions. Also, the DPAHC provides legal assurance that the patient's wishes will be carried out and that doctors who follow the directives in the DPAHC form will also be legally protected. Unlike the living will, the DPAHC allows the patient to designate the proxy who will serve as the patient's trusted interpreter of the patient's wishes and act on his or her behalf when the patient is no longer able to do so. This gives the patient greater assurance that his or her wishes will be respected.

The DPAHC is a dramatic legal step forward protecting the well-established principle of autonomy giving the patient the right to refuse medical treatment. It gives medical practitioners greater certainty of the patient's wishes in hard decisions about treatment preferences, and it provides these practitioners and the health care facility a substantial measure of protection from civil and criminal liability when relying on a proxy decision in cases of terminal illness.[20]

Best Interest Standard

While living wills may be very helpful in assisting in proxy representation, we are still left with the need for some guiding principles to help the proxy when the patient's wishes have never been expressed, informally or formally. In these instances, the "best interests" standard becomes the guiding principle. It presumes that the mentally incapable patient would want what most reasonable people would want in similar circumstances.

But what do most "reasonable people" want? One prominent interpretation calls for assessing whether the anticipated benefits of the proposed treatment outweigh the burdens of the treatment under the present set of circumstances. The President's

Commission recognizes that a certain element of subjectivity is inevitable on the part of the proxy in defining the patient's best interests and weighing benefits and burdens. Yet it does identify some factors which a proxy must take into account when assessing whether a treatment would be in the patient's best interests. It identifies such factors as the relief of suffering, the preservation or restoration of functioning, the quality as well as the extent of life sustained, and the impact of the decision on the patient's loved ones, since most people do have an important interest in the well-being of their families or close associates.[21]

Some of the most difficult proxy judgments pertain to cases of severely handicapped infants whose lives could be saved (e.g., some cases of spina bifida, Down's Syndrome with intestinal blockage), but with a burden some would consider too great to bear. Veatch rejects proxy refusal on the grounds that the burden is too great to others. Burden to the patient is the only legitimate grounds for refusal. An example of reasonable refusal based on burden to the patient would be the need for repeated surgeries throughout one's lifetime, such as in the case of repairing congenital heart malformations or making shunt corrections.[22]

Robert Veatch has collaborated with Richard McCormick to offer some further guiding principles for deciding on behalf of patients with impaired mental capacity.[23] They find the necessity for such guiding principles to be underscored by the reasoning behind the judgments made in the Quinlan, Saikewicz and Fox cases. Their proposal argues that something more than the principle of self-determination must be provided to guide decision-making. Their first principle is the principle of patient benefit. This means that the proxy must judge in the patient's best interests when deciding to withhold or withdraw medical treatment. The second principle is that of familial autonomy, or familial self-determination, which says that the family or family surrogate (like a religious community or superior) shall decide in the patient's best interests.

> The family is normally in the best position to judge the real interests of the incompetent patient. They know his or her life style, preferences, and values. The family knows those treat-

ments that might be particularly disturbing and those that the patient may have accepted without distress in the past.

Second, however (and we think this is the more important reason), our society places great value on the family. The family is a basic moral community affirmed to have not only the rights but responsibilities in determining how best to serve the interests of its incompetent members.[24]

McCormick and Veatch would like to make familial autonomy the locus of power and control in the exercise of proxy rights as long as family judgments stay with the limits of what is a reasonable expression of the patient's best interests. The President's Commission[25] and James Childress also endorse familial autonomy.[26] Like McCormick and Veatch, they do not hold the priority of the family as final. If the familial judgment deviates from the patient's interests and exalts its own interest, for example, then the community assumes responsibility for making a good decision. The community may be represented by friends of the patient, medical professionals, an ethics committee in the hospital, or the courts, if ultimately necessary.[27]

Paul Ramsey objects to "best interests" proposals for proxy judgments because of the danger of imposing some quality-of-life standards through the influence of the proxy's "values." He argues from the point of view of his medical indications policy narrowly construed in physiological terms. His chief plea is this: "The tests for telling whether to discontinue treatments should be clinical or physiological ones (if these are the proper words for my meaning), not anyone's 'values.'"[28] The judgment of the "medical indications" is the proper domain of the physician. Therefore, because the primary factors are medical rather than valuational, medical personnel have priority in decisions for the mentally incapacitated.[29] McCormick wonders, however, whether Ramsey already assumes a set of values in the guise of his medical indications policy since he "values" sustaining the life of a non-dying patient regardless of its quality.[30]

These are some guidelines for the many instances in which the question "Who decides?" must be answered. In the case of the patient who has the mental capacity to understand his or her medical situation, the presumption is given in favor of the patient's reasonable requests. Most everyone seems to agree on that. In the case of the patient who lacks this capacity, our first concern should be the best interest of the patient. This means doing what he or she would want if mentally capable of choosing. If the patient's wishes have been made known, these wishes ought to be respected. If the patient has never been mentally capable of understanding and choosing, then we are left with some hard choices. Reasonable person standards, familial autonomy ensuring patient benefit, and a medical indications policy provide some guidance for prudence to operate.

Truth-Telling

The focus of the discussion of "Who decides?" was on the locus of power and control for decisions pertaining to the sick person's life. If control and power are to remain with the person whose life is in question, then that person needs proper information upon which to base his or her consent to treatment, or to being a patient at all. Truth-telling, then, is the flip side of "Who decides?" Both share the underlying values of patient well-being and autonomy, or self-determination. Moreover, the truth must be told if physicians and patients are to maintain a therapeutic relationship marked by trust and cooperation. But how much "truth" is necessary for a patient to be properly informed? Is deception ever permissible?

Parentalistic Deception

Patients have long complained about deception and incomplete disclosure of information in medicine. Two recent novels, Cornelius and Kathryn Ryan's *A Private Battle* [31] and Martha Lear's *Heartsounds,* [32] give extensive personal accounts of coping with terminal illness for four or more years. One of the persistent themes in each account is deception, incomplete disclosure, and the withholding of relevant information which the dying husbands would need to take charge of their lives. Perhaps Leo Tolstoy speaks for many dying patients through his character of Ivan

Illych in his classic short story, *The Death of Ivan Illych,* when he writes:

> What troubled Ivan Illych most was the deception, the lie, which for some reason they all accepted, that he was not dying but was simply ill, and that he only need keep quiet and undergo a treatment and then something very good would result. . . . This deception tortured him—their not wishing to admit what they all knew and what he knew, but wanting to lie to him concerning his terrible condition, and wishing and forcing him to participate in that lie. Those lies . . . were a terrible agony for Ivan Illych.[33]

In the Ryans', Lears' and Tolstoy accounts, deception or incomplete disclosure was always done in the patient's interest. These accounts clearly show how the Hippocratic tradition has supported the "therapeutic privilege" to deceive by giving greater stress to the duty to do no harm and to the responsibility to do what is in the best interest of the patient than it has given to the duty to tell the truth. In the traditional conception of the physician-patient relationship, the duty to tell the truth has been subordinate to physicians doing what they think best for their patients by withholding information they think would probably do harm. From this perspective, truthfulness depends on its usefulness to the patient's well-being. An attitude of "what you don't know won't hurt you" prevails over giving the patient the freedom to exercise self-determination. By exercising the "therapeutic privilege"[34] to restrict or withhold disclosure, physicians control the patient's access to information according to the physicians' perception of what the patient needs, regardless of what the patient wants.[35] Robert Weir summarizes this parentalistic perspective and its influence on truth-telling:

> Working out of this perspective of medical [parentalism], physicians sometimes think they know more about a patient's needs, interests, and emotional stability than the patient does and withhold potentially damaging information to protect the patient from possibly undergoing an emotional catastrophe. As controllers of vital information, they conclude that the

withholding of all (or at least a significant part) of such information is often in "the best interest of the patient."[36]

Sissela Bok, in her extensive study of deception, *Lying,* examines and finds wanting the three major arguments supporting deception: "that truthfulness is impossible; that patients do not want bad news; and that truthful information harms them."[37] Similarly, Robert Veatch examines and finds wanting various forms of these arguments under what he calls the "Big Lie."[38] Sissela Bok draws a conclusion that fits both her own and Veatch's analysis:

> The common view that many patients cannot understand, do not want, and may be harmed by, knowledge of their condition, and that lying to them is either morally neutral or even to be recommended, must be set aside.[39]

Bok, Childress, Veatch and Weir would join in characterizing the strength of the duty to tell the truth as a *prima facie* obligation.[40] This means, other things being equal, that the presumption rests in favor of telling the truth and that the burden of proof must be borne by the one who intends to deceive. Sissela Bok spells out what this burden of proof entails:

> They must show why they fear a patient may be harmed or how they know that another cannot cope with the truthful knowledge. A decision to deceive must be seen as a very unusual step, to be talked over with colleagues and others who participate in the care of the patient. Reasons must be set forth and debated, alternatives weighed carefully. At all times, the correct information must go to *someone* closely related to the patient.[41]

Informed Consent

The principles of respect for persons and a patient's autonomy, or self-determination, require that we not lie or deceive patients, but that we disclose information that will enable them to be in control of their lives again. Since one of the greatest fears of being sick is the fear of losing autonomy or control of one's life, Dr. Eric Cassell believes that the primary function of medicine is to preserve autonomy.[42] Some control can be restored to the patient by providing information which enables the patient to make decisions about his or her own health and life. A terminally ill person, for example, who is not informed that his or her illness is incurable would not be given a chance to put his or her life in order and to make decisions about the ways he or she wants to live while dying.

The duty to disclose information regarding the patient's current medical status, the nature of proposed procedures along with their benefits and risks, as well as alternative procedures together with a professional opinion as to which is best is expressed in the rule of "informed consent."[43] Warren Reich has effectively argued that if informed consent is going to respect a patient's autonomy, then it must go beyond these minimalist requirements of disclosing relevant clinical facts to include a discussion of the relevant values which the physician and patient hold. Without a discussion of values, neither the physician nor the patient is being treated as a moral person, a truly moral judgment about appropriate care is impossible, and the goals of the physician-patient relationship are reduced to curing the disease while excluding the larger concerns of caring for the patient.[44] The President's Commission wants to see informed consent become not only a moral and legal formality but also a process of shared decision-making between patients and health care providers.[45]

Benedict Ashley regards the right and obligation of informed consent as fundamental to all medical-ethical decisions.

> I cannot insist too strongly that the physician has no right to decide for the patient whether or how life is to be prolonged by medical art. The doctor's right and responsibility extends only to informing the patient truthfully about his or her terminal condition and the possible ways in which this can be handled medically. The choice among these is the patient's, although this choice cannot be made prudently without honest and substantially complete medical information; yet it cannot be done on this information alone.[46]

Paul Ramsey regards this consent requirement as a canon of loyalty expressing the faithfulness claims of the physician-patient

relationship. For him it has the strength of a "practical absolute."
This means that while we cannot theoretically rule out the possibility of an exception, it is still "a rule of the highest human
loyalty that ought not in practice be held open to significant
future revision."[47] Informed consent is a farce if information is
distorted or withheld. It is fulfilled not only by giving the information a "reasonable patient"[48] would want to know, but also by
disclosing whatever the patient wants to know in such a way, at
such a time, and in such proper increments that it can be
understood.[49]

Attitudes Toward Truth-Telling

In working out what informed consent implies, significant
attention has been given to the importance of truth-telling. The
attitude toward truth-telling has dramatically changed over the
last twenty-five years, if not in practice, at least in policy. In 1961,
Donald Oken's study of the policy of physicians for disclosing a
diagnosis of cancer reported that 88% of the physicians surveyed
had a policy of not telling the patient.[50] The 1979 report of Dennis Novack and his colleagues shows that 98% of the physicians
surveyed had a policy of telling.[51]

What accounts for the shift toward disclosure? The research
of Veatch and Tai shows that a host of factors account for the
shift. For example, between 1961–1979 we have experienced a
general pro-truth movement in our culture. In the medical world,
we have experienced a shift in our beliefs about the benefit and
harm caused by disclosure. No longer is disclosure considered to
be automatically harmful. Also, a shift has occurred in the social
structure of medicine so that the physician-patient relationship
reflects less the parentalistic patient-protective patterns of physicians and includes more patient-centered patterns of patient
involvement, especially in chronic disease patients. This
accounts for the increased attention being given to patient autonomy, the right to self-determination and the right to be informed
so as to give consent. Also, the physician's perception of what is
standard practice has shifted from what the consensus of colleagues would favor to what a reasonable person would want to
know in order to make an informed decision. Finally, the bureau-

cratization of health care makes disclosure more important since the patient can be easily confused by the mixed messages coming from the multiple personnel involved in any one patient's case.[52]

The dilemma of whether to tell or not to tell seems to arise from the moral conflict between the patient's right to know the truth and the patient's welfare if the truth cannot be handled. Two moral perspectives appear in these policy changes. One perspective reflects the consequentialist thinking of the Hippocratic tradition which aims to benefit the patient and do no harm. This perspective grants information because, on balance, more patients receive benefit than harm from being informed. The other perspective reflects deontological thinking. The physician discloses information to honor the patient's right to the information and to fulfill the physician's duty to tell the truth.[53]

These two perspectives help us to decide whether to tell or not to tell. If we decide on the basis of consequences, we need to calculate the risks and benefits of disclosing critical information of a fatal illness and then decide whether telling or not telling would contribute to the greatest benefit of the patient. Deception would be justified if it achieved the desirable end of maintaining the patient's hope. But if the patient is to be respected as the locus of decision-making, then we need to determine what the patient wants to know and disclose the information necessary for the patient to make a reasonably informed decision about his or her own care, even at the risk of causing some emotional anxiety or psychological harm.

Withholding Information

If we are going to grant that the presumption lies in favor of telling the truth, as most authors do, under what conditions can withholding information ever be justified? Robert Weir favors the presumption but does not absolutize the duty to tell the truth, since this would take away the freedom of physicians as responsible moral agents. For Weir, the physician is obliged to tell the truth

> unless there is a conflicting and stronger duty which takes precedence in a particular clinical context. The "unless clause"

does not weaken the claim that truth-telling with patients is a moral obligation applicable to all physicians. It merely acknowledges that there could be exceptional circumstances (e.g., a clear, indisputable indication that truth-telling would lead to an attempted suicide by the patient) in which another obligation to a particular patient would override the physician's truth-telling responsibility.[54]

The President's Commission discusses five possible situations in which full disclosure is not desirable or required. These are cases of (1) medical interventions directed by law, such as immunization for public health; (2) emergencies; (3) mental incapacity, such as when a proxy needs to decide; (4) waivers, such as when a patient delegates decision-making authority to another; (5) well circumscribed instances of professionals exercising therapeutic privilege to withhold information.[55]

Robert Veatch has explored other possibilities to great effect. For instance, can withholding information be justified if the family requests it? Not in the case of a patient with sufficient mental capacity to decide, says Veatch.

Patients have both a right and a duty to consent to their medical treatment based upon reasonable knowledge of their medical conditions. This right and duty cannot be waived on behalf of a mentally competent patient by a spouse, children, or relatives. This, of course, does not apply to the legally incompetent patient.[56]

Does the patient's own request justify withholding? Based on the limitations of judging from the patient-benefit perspective, and based on the principles of respect for the person and self-determination, Veatch would favor respecting the request of a patient for withholding information in most cases. The instances when this request need not be respected are those in which the welfare of others is at stake, especially those who stand in a relationship of special obligation to the patient, such as children.[57] Veatch further points out that those who stand in a relationship of special obligation to others have the moral duty to seek information that is useful to them. Veatch offers a rule of practice to guide instances of a patient's request for withholding information which protects the image of the medical profession and the patient's self-determination: "Always tell the truth except in those cases where the patient has clearly requested not to know and where others would not suffer from the withholding."[58] James Childress would agree: "People may choose to live in ignorance of their condition and fate, as long as others are not adversely affected."[59] Out of respect for persons, their freedom to choose their styles of living and dying should be respected.

What if disclosing information would produce overwhelmingly negative consequences? In the extreme instance, withholding would be morally tolerated. But Veatch believes that such instances would be extremely rare. The prospect of some great negative consequences indicates, not total withholding, but a policy of moderating what is told for the time being until the patient has passed through a crisis and is able to receive the information more appropriately.[60]

Manner of Disclosure

This leads to a final consideration under truth-telling, and that is the manner of disclosure. Out of a respect for persons, truth-telling does not mean that the patient must be told abruptly about a serious diagnosis. Dr. Cicely Saunders, who runs the famous St. Christopher's Hospice in England, describes the sensitivity and understanding that are needed:

> Every patient needs an explanation of his illness that will be understandable and convincing to him if he is to cooperate in his treatment or be relieved of the burden of unknown fears. This is true whether it is a question of giving a diagnosis in a hopeful situation or of confirming a poor prognosis.
>
> The fact that a patient does not ask does not mean that he has no questions. One visit or one talk is rarely enough. It is only by waiting and listening that we can gain an idea of what we should be saying. . . .
>
> The alternatives are not merely silence, bland denial, or stark fatal truth. There are many different truths just as there are

many ways of imparting them. We have to try and learn to give the one the individual needs at that moment in the simplest and kindest way we can offer it, leaving him the choice to take it or leave it as he wishes.[61]

Similarly, Dr. Elisabeth Kübler-Ross gives this response to the question, "Should every patient be told that he is dying?"

No patient should be told that he is dying. I do not encourage people to force patients to face their own death when they are not ready for it. Patients should be told that they are seriously ill. When they are ready to bring up the issue of death and dying, we should answer them, we should listen to them, and we should hear the questions, but you do not go around telling patients they are dying and depriving them of a glimpse of hope that they may need in order to live until they die.[62]

Truth-telling is a fundamental moral responsibility of those who care for the dying. The presumption always lies in favor of telling the truth, and the burden of proof falls on anyone who would advocate withholding critical information. Even if the patient does not directly ask for information, the best policy for respecting persons and for enhancing autonomy is to disclose the information that a reasonable person would want to know. Of course, the manner, time, and increments of information need to be considered in a sensitive way. The responsibility to tell the truth is not resolved in a moment, and is rarely a matter simply of direct expression. More truthfully, it extends over time. Perhaps the best policy is to be guided by the patient's verbal and non-verbal cues as to how much, what, when, and how to tell. The process of communication should be sensitive to the person's condition and wishes and should be couched in a language understandable to the patient. Above all, truth-telling must reassure those who are suffering that they will not be abandoned when they most need help.

Hospice: A Concept of Terminal Care

A third dimension in the ethics of caring for the dying pertains to our obligations of providing a decent death. In the midst of all the diversity surrounding the discussion of the ethical issues and positions pertaining to euthanasia, a general consensus does prevail that our obligation to the irreversibly dying patient turns from curing to caring. Opinions about the forms which this care ought to take may vary, but the opinion that we ought to provide the dying patient with a decent death is unanimous. One particular form of caring for the dying which has institutional dimensions, and which is beginning to receive a great deal more public attention, is the hospice form of terminal care.[63] "Hospice," properly understood, refers not to a building, but to a concept of care. How does hospice fit into this larger discussion of euthanasia and the ethical considerations in the care of the dying patient?

The Hospice Concept

Hospice in America is a transplant from England. The modern hospice movement started in 1967 when Dr. Cecily Saunders opened the now famous St. Christopher's Hospice in London. The work of Dr. Saunders and St. Christopher's Hospice has become the model of modern hospice care. The hospice movement emerged in America in the early 1970s, and the first U.S. hospice—Hospice, Inc. (now Connecticut Hospice, Inc.) in New Haven, Connecticut—opened in 1974. The National Hospice Organization has formulated the following definition of hospice and hospice care:

> Hospice is a medically directed multidisciplinary program providing skilled care of an appropriate nature for terminally ill patients and their families to live as fully as possible until the time of death—helps relieve symptoms and provide support during the distress (physical, psychological, spiritual, social, economic) that may occur during the course of disease, dying, and bereavement.[64]

Three central principles of care are enshrined in the philosophy of hospice: (1) to treat the patient as a person, which means involving the patient in discussions about his or her illness and symptoms; (2) to control the symptoms and pain of the terminal illness in order to enable the dying person to live his or her last months, weeks, or days as comfortably and as fully as possible free from pain and fear and as much in control as possible; (3) to care for the family not only while the patient is dying but also through the mourning process.[65]

In Britain, hospices are an established part of the health-care system and funded by the National Health Service and by donations. In the U.S., hospice is still emerging, and funding remains one of its great problems.[66] Hospice programs in the U.S. began as operations to provide supportive terminal care to persons in their own homes. Presently, five general types of hospice programs make up the more than eight hundred programs in various stages of development in the U.S.: (1) free standing hospice facilities providing inpatient service along with home care (e.g., Connecticut Hospice, Inc.); (2) home-care agencies (e.g., Hospice of Marin in Kentfield, California); (3) hospice care units within a hospital (e.g., Hospice Group of Bellin Memorial Hospital, Green Bay, Wisconsin); (4) roving hospice teams working with dying patients wherever they are located (e.g., St. Luke's Hospital Center, New York City); (5) hospice programs with a hospital and medical school affiliation (e.g., St. John's Hospice in Springfield, Illinois).[67] In whatever the setting, hospice care-givers are committed to satisfying the individual life styles and the physical, social, legal, psychological and spiritual needs of both family and patient.

The Challenges of Hospice

One challenge to the hospice movement is the referral of appropriate patients by physicians and hospitals.[68] Hospice care is appropriate for patients for whom death is imminent and who do not want to fight death by using aggressive measures. These patients have decided that present efforts to bring about a cure are no longer beneficial. Such a dying person, though beyond cure, still wants and has the moral right to quality care in order to live well while dying. Hospice care for the terminally ill does not seek to hurry death, but to help the dying live as comfortably as possible until death comes as a result of the illness that is now beyond cure. In the hospice program of care, important relationships are preserved, the dying patient and family have a voice in planning care, and the dying is kept as pain-free as possible.

Hospice care is not anti-technological. Though it may not use the technology of respirators, risky surgery, IVs, transfusions, or any other artificial life-support measures (except when necessary to relieve discomfort), it uses technology in the service of the dying by blending methods of pain and symptom control with human warmth and personal support. At St. Christopher's, for example, "the total care of the dying patient refers not only to the medical management of symptoms but more importantly to the concept that anything that produces distress or pain for the dying patient or the family is the concern of the Hospice."[69]

The basic philosophy of pain control in hospice care is to prevent pain from occurring rather than to control it once it appears. This is accomplished through the regular (not "p.r.n.," i.e., "as needed") administration of the now famous "Brompton Cocktail," or some similar pain relief medication.[70] The goal is to maintain the right dosage of medication to relieve pain but without causing sedation which would cancel the benefits of pain-free living.

The question of addiction obviously arises at this point. Abuse of pain control in the form of drug addiction could be devastating to the hospice movement. Cecily Saunders, however, does not find that drug abuse or addiction is an issue in the clinical setting of the hospice. For one reason, the use of narcotics is under clinical supervision and scheduled for pain-relief, not for euphoric effect. Furthermore, drug abuse and addiction is held in check by a well-balanced program of drug dosage together with a multi-disciplinary approach to symptomatic care which recognizes pain relief as more than the administration of drugs.[71]

Hospice care for the terminally ill is not an alternative to health care, but a supplement to it. Hospice supplements the medical needs of the dying patient with needs that medicine alone cannot provide. Hospice care does not reduce terminal care simply to removing artificial life-support systems. In hospice care, when these kinds of supports are withheld or removed, other kinds of supports take their place—such as a family environment and legal, spiritual, economic and social support.

Moral Dimensions of Hospice

As an extension of health care, hospice care shares the moral base of health care and upholds the same fundamental principles of respect for persons, self-determination, and patient benefit. The hospice movement does not support euthanasia; rather it does recognize the general validity of the moral significance of the distinction between killing (directly inducing death) and allowing the patient to die by withholding life-supportive measures in the proper circumstances. But in the case of the dying, this distinction gives way to a calculation of the burden and benefit that certain therapies bring to the patient. This puts the hospice approach in line with the moral consensus that defends the personal integrity and freedom of the dying patient to refuse treatment which serves no purpose other than to prolong the dying process, or which causes more burden than can be justified by the benefits. In short, therapeutic recommendations in hospice care revolve around their expected effectiveness for the dying patient. The hospice approach makes the practical application of this principle easier by enabling a more personalized relationship between the physician, patient and family where communication is frank but sensitive.[72]

Furthermore, hospice care can resolve many of the ethical dilemmas faced when caring for the dying in other environments, especially ones which easily arise in acute care facilities dominated by sophisticated medical technology. The sophisticated technology of modern medicine often provokes rather than alleviates moral problems related to care for the dying—problems of basic moral emotions like sentiment, and conflicts of conscience: who decides, to tell or not to tell, to use or not to use sophisticated aggressive treatment. Hospice care avoids these sorts of ethical dilemmas because many ethical decisions are made in advance. For example, entering a hospice program means that no aggressive treatment will be used. Also, truth-telling problems are avoided because hospice patients already know they are dying. In hospice the basic moral emotions, like sentiment, which family, friends and care-givers share, are expressed by accompanying the dying. Hospice care seems to be an opportunity to carry out in deed our moral responsibility to help the dying live well while dying and to die a decent death.

5
The Moral Art of Terminal Care

At the beginning of this book I asked, "Should medicine do all that it can?" The decision about whether to forego or to administer life-prolonging treatment is one way of specifying that general question. This book's summary of the moral discussion of euthanasia and its related issues shows that we have no single indicator that invariably serves to determine what that decision will be. We can say, however, that several factors must work together, a few of which have been given prominence by many of the authorities cited in this book. These are: (1) knowledge of the patient, including a knowledge of the patient's value history, which entails at least the patient's beliefs, fears, hopes, life plans and the value placed on life; (2) the patient's expressed or reasonably implied wishes for treatment when in a terminal condition; (3) the burden the patient must bear by way of physical discomfort or physical and mental impairment as well as the burden (financial or otherwise) on the patient's family; (4) the hope of reversing an illness and restoring the patient to a reasonable level of well-being; (5) the proxy (usually the family) judgment that should become the guiding word when the patient cannot or has not expressed his or her wishes about treatment when in a terminal condition. Each of us may rank these factors differently in their order of importance to us for making a decision about treatment when in a terminal condition. Our ranking will reflect our basic moral character and vision formed by underlying convictions about health and life.

135

A survey of principles, issues and positions pertaining to a specific medical-moral problem such as this book represents, together with this brief identification of factors and the need to rank them for making a treatment decision, can easily distort the nature and scope of medical ethics. Medical ethics involves more than drawing distinctions, marshalling principles, or ranking pertinent factors in order to analyze and solve a particular moral dilemma. Medical ethics taken as a whole also includes considerations of the character of the health care professional, the patient and the community which sustains the health care system.[1] The moral commitments of these moral agents can only partially be expressed in principles and factors like those considered in this book. Moral commitments also involve convictions which shape our vision and character and dispose us to act according to principles and ideals. This book has not adequately highlighted convictions, character and vision which make medicine a moral art by shaping the nature of our care, sustaining it even in the face of death, and disposing us to act in accord with moral principles and ideals.

Stanley Hauerwas has argued that the real moral crisis in contemporary medicine is a crisis of convictions and not a crisis of problems resulting from the developments of scientific medicine.[2] His argument challenges us to ask, "Do we have the convictions which help fashion a vision of caring for one another with a sufficient sense of our physical and moral limits? Do we have the character based on these convictions to sustain our efforts to care in the face of death?" These are challenging questions. They cannot be addressed adequately in this concluding statement, though some steps can be taken.

This concluding statement, then, does not intend to provide a super-theory which incorporates all aspects of the moral issues already considered, nor does it intend to be a comprehensive theory with which to criticize all that has been surveyed. This concluding statement has a modest purpose. It intends to identify and briefly elaborate four convictions which give shape to our care for the dying and dispose us to act according to certain principles and ideals which contribute to the moral art of terminal care. In this way, this concluding statement can not only serve to focus some of the main features of the discussion pertaining to the moral responsibilities in prolonging life, but it can also serve as a permission for being a little less fearful and nervous about making decisions that pertain to the treatment and care of the dying.

As the previous chapters clearly show, "dying" and "terminally ill" are not ironclad categories of a technical sort that can be ascertained by clear and precise criteria. Rather, they are descriptive terms for patients whose illness is progressing toward and likely to cause death within what is to the patient a very short time. Unlike the "hopelessly" ill patient whose situation is stable and not progressing toward death (e.g., the severely demented, or quadriplegic), the "terminally ill" patient cannot be stabilized. Treatment cannot restore the terminally ill to health. Any further medical intervention would only prolong the dying process. The difficulty of diagnosis and the possibility of surprise recoveries make determining a case of irreversibly "dying" or "terminal illness" difficult. But generally we can make a reasonable estimation that a person will die in a short time. This "reasonable" estimation is sufficient for making good moral judgments.

1. Life is not an absolute good that must be preserved at all costs, and death is not an absolute evil to be avoided at all costs.

This basic conviction about life and death encourages us to find our way between two extremes. The one extreme is physicalist vitalism which wants to do everything possible to secure the maximum length of physical life regardless of the dying person's condition. The other extreme is utilitarian pessimism which wants to end physical life when it becomes frustrating, useless or burdensome. Our attitudes toward life and its meaning shape our attitudes toward death and its meaning. In fact, our moral judgments of the various alternatives we have when dealing with the terminally ill can be seen as an extension of our attitude toward life and death. For the Christian, the attitude toward life and death is shaped by the religious beliefs of the Christian faith.

According to Christian belief, we live in a world of grace. Everything comes to us as a gift to be cherished and shared and not as a possession to be hoarded or abused. Life is such a gift, a precious one at that. Novelist Chaim Potok, in *My Name Is Asher Lev,* has written well about the fundamental attitude toward life which sees life as a gift from God. In the following scene, Asher Lev recalls a childhood memory of the way his father once looked at a bird lying on its side against the curb near their house:

> "Is it dead, Papa?" I was six and could not bring myself to look at it.
> "Yes," I heard him say in a sad and distant way.
> "Why did it die?"
> "Everything that lives must die."
> "Everything?"
> "Yes."
> "You, too, Papa? And Mama?"
> "Yes."
> "And me?"
> "Yes," he said. Then he added in Yiddish, "But may it be only after you live a long and good life, my Asher."
> I couldn't grasp it. I forced myself to look at the bird. Everything alive would one day be as still as that bird?
> "Why?" I asked.
> "That's the way the Ribbono Shel Olom made His world, Asher."
> "Why?"
> "So life would be precious, Asher. Something that is yours forever is never precious."
> "I'm frightened, Papa."
> "Come. We'll go home and have our Shabbos meal and sing zemiros to the Ribbono Shel Olom."[3]

Human life is God's creation and our task, God's gift to us and our responsibility. Our belief in God as Creator and Sustainer of life calls us to relate to life according to our understanding of its relation to God's love.[4] This belief engenders an attitude of reverence for life as a precious creation of God for which we are responsible. This attitude of reverence enables us to hold fast to the principle of the sanctity of life. It tempers destructive intrusions into life and demands good reasons for any interventions into the process of life. Human life, as God's gift and our responsibility, is not properly reverenced by putting others at the disposal of our whims, ambitions or desires to serve some utilitarian end.

Moreover, our belief in God as Creator and Sustainer evokes a presumption in favor of sustaining life. Even though we are the created and not the Creator, our human glory is that we can transcend some of the limits of our nature by cooperating with the God who continues to act in our history and who opens new possibilities for human well-being. We must transcend our limitations as well as consent to them. This tension of being both creature and co-agent with God will always be unresolved for us. While our life and our hope have reasonable limits, we must not sacrifice life as long as we have reasonable hope for its well-being. And we must not sacrifice our hope when life has reached its reasonable limits.

Physical life remains the fundamental condition for all other values of human life and sets limits within which we must work to promote its well-being. We show reverence for this gift of life, and give thanks to God for it, by doing whatever is required for the healthy functioning of our bodies. But our belief in God as Creator and Sustainer does not demand an idolatrous reverence which makes physical life an absolute value. In the case of the terminally ill, dying well is really living well with a dying body, a body which has lost its power of recovery. This is quite different from the seriously ill but not dying. They still have a body capable of recovery and are morally responsible for doing what is required to recover. When we live with bodies capable of recovery, we can live with hope that sees every moment, even moments of pain, fear, despair, or struggle, as occasions for growth as persons. But the terminally ill have no hope in this capacity for creative living. Their hope is in eternal life. The presumption in favor of sustaining life yields to (only) caring for the dying when physical life has reached its reasonable limits and creative living becomes impossible. Any further treatment to prolong life then would only be too burdensome and without benefit to the dying person's well-being.

Death, in the Christian view, is not the absolute evil. The death-resurrection of Jesus Christ has deprived death of its power to destroy us. A Christian attitude toward death is that it has been transformed by Jesus Christ. The resurrection of Jesus has drawn the sting out of death. Death for the Christian is not an absurd departure into nothingness, but death is coming home to God. If death were annihilation, then the Crucified would be the symbol of what life is all about. But for the Christian, the Resurrected One is the symbol of life. Moreover, death as annihilation is an affront to the experience of the value of persons and to the reality of human and divine love. Our belief in immortality and eternal life means that the value of the person continues beyond death. Those whom we know and love are too valuable and precious to believe that they are annihilated by death.[5] And, as St. Paul says, "Nothing can separate us from the love of God," not even death (Rom 8:38).

From this perspective, death acquires a different place on our scale of values. It is not the dark enemy with a brutal power of annihilation. While struggling with one's health can be meaningful up to a point, and suffering can be a purifying agent and occasion for creative living up to a point, struggling against death at all costs is nonsense. Death is not so much destruction as change. "Life is changed, not ended," says the preface of the Catholic funeral Mass. In this view, death is less a diminishing and a perishing and more of a consummation and a fulfillment. We need not cling fearfully to life as our final possession. In death, we come home to God as the fullness of our lives.

2. The patient's free and informed choice ought to determine whether or not life-sustaining therapy will be used.

The increased use of technology in medicine, rising costs and the federal government's efforts to control costs, plus increased public involvement in health care through legislative and judicial action, are having a profound effect on the structure of the health care system.[6] Because of these influences, patients are having a more difficult time retaining control over their lives, illness and death, thus forcing a new look at the relationship between the patient and the health care professionals. For example, the mere presence of advanced technology entices physicians to pre-program treatments and to use all the means available for them. In such a situation, doing less, when less may even be too much, becomes very difficult for physicians. Will care for the terminally ill be seen in light of these impersonal forces or in light of the personal prerogatives of the patient?

The long-standing conviction of the medical profession is that decision-making ought to be controlled by the patient-physician-family relationship and tailored to each individual case. The health care system today faces the challenge of finding an appropriate balance of responsibilities within this relationship. One extreme is medical parentalism which makes the patient thoroughly dependent on the physician's judgment of what is in the medical best interest of the patient. This extreme shows little respect for patient autonomy. The other extreme is patient sovereignty. This maximizes patient control by transforming the physician into a hired technician practicing under the directions of the patient. This extreme treats the physician as a value-free moral automaton. A balanced approach would seek to involve the patient in decisions about his or her life and death, while also respecting the competence, freedom and values of the physician.[7]

The kind of treatment and level of care provided a terminally ill patient (or any other patient, for that matter) ought to respect the self-determination of the patient with sufficient mental capacity to choose according to his or her view of well-being. Each person has different needs and concerns during the final period of life. The moral question we face in deciding on prolongation-of-life treatments is whether the continued bodily life of the patient is of value to this patient. This is not to ask whether it is of any value to the family, to society, or to medical science. But is it of value to this patient? Living a little longer has a different meaning for different people. Some people, for whom every moment of life is valuable, would consider aggressive treatment appropriate. For others, life without some desired level of physical and mental ability is worthless. Once such a person goes beyond this desired level, any further treatment is too burdensome. For some, a moderate degree of suffering may be an avenue of religious experience or an important means of personal growth. For still others, this same suffering is frightening and too much for them to bear.

Helping patients with differing views of reasonable health and well-being requires sensitivity and wisdom. For dying patients, who are ultimately losing control over their lives, maintaining control over decisions still to be made is very important. In order to respond to this need, all those who care for the dying need not only sensitivity and wisdom, but also skills for communicating with the dying patient and the family so that decisions about aggressive treatment, institutional arrangements and symptom control remain with the patient as much as possible. In all cases of a terminally ill, informed, and mentally capable patient, the presumption lies in favor of the patient's request. The terminally ill patient with sufficient mental capacity to understand his or her medical situation and to make choices has the right to refuse life-prolonging treatment, and this request ought to be honored. For patients without such a capacity and who have not expressed personal wishes, we need to ask at least whether continued bodily life offers them any opportunity to participate in human experiences and life-enriching relationships with God and with others.

In order for the terminally ill patient to participate as fully as possible in making decisions, he or she needs to be properly informed. A trusting, cooperative, therapeutic relationship between the patient and the health care professionals, as well as the patient's right to self-determination, requires that truthful information be communicated. The burden of the proof not to disclose falls on those who believe that the patient cannot cope with the information. The research evidence shows that the patient is better off knowing the truth about a diagnosis and prognosis. Moreover, withholding the truth about a terminal illness effectively isolates the patient at a time when truthful sharing and emotional support are most needed. Disclosure of a diagnosis and prognosis of a terminal illness should occur as soon as this information is firm and ought to be communicated in a language the patient can understand, in increments the patient can assimilate, and in a manner that does not destroy the patient's hope.

The health care professionals need to remain open and available to further discussion of this information and need to provide emotional support which does not leave the patient abandoned.

Ideally, the patient's preference for treatment, especially for the refusal of treatment, is made when the diagnosis is clear and the patient is well-informed. Since circumstances are often less than ideal, the patient's capacity for such a judgment needs to be properly assessed. For example, emergencies which do not allow time for discussion, or moments of intractable pain or depression, would be some conditions that would hinder a patient's capacity to make a judgment about refusal of treatment. However, only when the patient's capacity is clearly lacking can others substitute their judgment for the patient's and override the refusal of treatment.

If a patient's capacity is progressively reduced and a proxy judgment must be made, then this judgment ought to come from the person previously selected by the patient to speak on his or her behalf. In the absence of such a person, the family usually best serves as proxy. The proxy judgment must rely on the previously expressed wishes of the patient, or, if that is lacking, on the patient's presumed desires. These can be determined most formally by using a living will or the legal document, Durable Power of Attorney for Health Care. In the absence of such a formal expression, the proxy can rely on what he or she knows of the patient's perspective on life and its meaning, as well as on the patient's values and aspirations.

3. Treatments that cannot reverse the terminal illness of a dying patient are not morally required.

The general consensus of the medical, moral and legal communities continues to be that the medical commitment to cure a disease or relieve suffering does not extend to the direct intervention to terminate life. However, a general consensus also recognizes that some patients exist in conditions where initiating or continuing life-support treatment will be of no benefit to the patient since it will not improve the prognosis of recovery. As long as reasonable hope of recovery prevails, the appropriate treatment ought to be sought. But when a patient reaches beyond that point of reasonable recovery, stopping treatment is morally the same as not starting it. In cases of irreversible illness, any justification for withholding treatment is sufficient for withdrawing it. Ironically, as the President's Commission explains, according to present practice greater justification is demanded for withholding treatment than for withdrawing it since the effect of a treatment is uncertain until it is tried. Once the therapy is in progress, its benefit, or lack of benefit, is clearly evident to support stopping or continuing the treatment.[8] This means, for example, that when a comatose patient who is being mechanically ventilated is sincerely judged to be irreversibly comatose, the ventilator obviously ceases to be a necessary treatment and may be removed because it cannot reverse the coma. Yet stopping treatment once begun may be emotionally difficult to do, even if one has moral justification for stopping it. Recall the struggle of the Quinlan family as a case in point.

If we follow a patient-centered approach to health care, we can understand what makes the condition of a dying patient different from an otherwise healthy patient with the same disease. The kind of medical treatment appropriate when a person has the hope of recovery ceases to have meaning when recovery is impossible. In such a situation, the patient, or proxy, has to judge if treatment is warranted on the basis of whether it will enable the patient to live in the best way possible. Consider a pneumonia victim, for example. For an otherwise healthy person, treating pneumonia is morally required since it carries the hope of restored health. For a dying cancer patient, however, treating the pneumonia prolongs the dying process so that the suffering the patient endures is an added and unnecessary burden.

Our decision-making for treatment of the terminally ill may be relieved of much fear and nervousness if we keep one basic question in mind: Will this patient be sufficiently restored to health to justify the burden the patient must endure, as well as the burden those who care for the patient must bear? Our answering this question will involve covering various check points. Technically, we need to know whether any treatments are available to curb the present course of an illness, and if those treatments are reasonably available. Socio-economically, we need to consider the available resources of the patient, the patient's family, the medical community and society. While the primary consideration of what is reasonable ought to be determined on the basis of what benefits the patient, those who care for the dying patient ought not to ignore their personal concerns as well. Benedict Ashley has expressed this concern well:

> Obviously, those acting in behalf of a patient are also making sacrifices of time, emotional strain, and money. Such sacrifices have reasonable limits. Consequently, it is by no means wrong for the family of a dying patient faced with the prospects of a prolongation of life by an expensive medical procedure to take this also into consideration in deciding whether such expenditures are proportionate to the benefit the patient will receive. Indeed, this is not contrary to the reasonable interests of the patient who would hardly wish his or her family to be uselessly burdened. Every good family attempts to consider the interests of every member, but, in the effort to do this, fairness demands that the resources of the family be shared by all and not exhausted on a single member.[9]

Morally, we are concerned with respecting and promoting the patient's well-being. This involves consulting moral principles which presumptively ought to be obeyed since they express the wisdom and experience of the moral community on what has led to sustaining human well-being. It also involves considering the patient's perspectives on life and its meaning, as well as the patient's aspirations and values. Legally, we want to be sure that the patient's rights are being protected. Psychologically, we want to be clear on our real motives for our decision (e.g., Do we have a great inheritance to gain if death comes quickly? Do we dislike the patient because of his or her handicap? etc.). Spiritually, we need to help the patient face the challenges to his or her sense of meaning and hope by seeing life within a larger context of meaning and direction beyond the immediate world of suffering and inevitable death.

4. Decisions to withhold or withdraw treatment ought to intensify efforts to comfort.

When the goals of medicine to preserve health and relieve suffering have reached their limit so that therapy becomes futile and pain moves beyond the bounds of being a purifying agent of one's spirit to become destructive of life, or when the patient's goal of actualizing human potential has reached its limit, the moral obligation is then to comfort the patient. Paul Ramsey expresses this obligation succinctly:

> We cease doing what was once called for and begin to do precisely what is called for now. We attend and company with him [or her] in this, his [or her] very own dying, rendering it as comfortable and dignified as possible.[10]

This means that we should not treat the hopelessly ill and dying as if they were curable. We provide health care to those who are curable, but we provide comfort care to those who are not. The dying are more in need of comfort and company than of treatment. Ramsey's imperative is in line with one of the key findings of Elisabeth Kübler-Ross who has insisted that the chief fear of the dying is not death but being isolated and abandoned while dying.

Comfort care for the clearly terminal phase of an illness may mean using some technical measures to ensure a person's comfort.[11] This may require giving a sufficient amount of pain relief medication at frequent intervals to keep pain at bay, or it may include using urethral catheterization to increase comfort. It also includes careful attention to proper positioning of the patient, skin care, oral hygiene, disguising disfigurement by creative use of bed clothes and sheets, and making preferred foods available. Comfort care in the clearly terminal phase of an illness may also mean discontinuing blood pressure readings, lab tests and X-rays which serve only to program more medical therapy. Also, antibiotics need not be administered for infection. Nutrition and water may be given or withheld depending on the patient's comfort and that of those who care for the patient. Fluffing a pillow, washing a brow, or gently uttering familiar prayers are also appropriate means of caring, and, late in a terminal illness, may be the only appropriate care. In every case, however, when death is near, everyone concerned about the patient should direct his or her energies toward providing the loving care that eases the burden of dying. This can be done by conduct better guided by the common sense of a loving heart than by an order from a courtroom judge.

Comfort care faces the limits of our existence and of our medical power to heal with a realism that does not despair. The moral art of comfort care teaches us to accept that medicine involves trade-offs. Not all trade-offs are happy ones. While we will readily take the benefits that medicine offers, we must also be willing to take the burdens and losses of its limits. At times these are hard losses and great burdens, especially when life is at stake. But we can live with these losses if we have sufficiently formed ourselves, our vision and our character, by the convictions of an Easter people who live by the story that death does not have the last word. Life does. Where there is love, there is life. Since we believe that nothing can separate us from the love of God, we live with the conviction that in God's love, death is not the victor. We have life.

Appendix:
Declaration on Euthanasia

Vatican Congregation for the Doctrine of the Faith
June 26, 1980

Introduction

The rights and values pertaining to the human person occupy an important place among the questions discussed today. In this regard, the Second Vatican Ecumenical Council solemnly reaffirmed the lofty dignity of the human person, and in a special way his or her right to life. The council therefore condemned crimes against life "such as any type of murder, genocide, abortion, euthanasia, or willful suicide" (Pastoral Constitution "Gaudium et Spes," no. 27).

More recently, the Sacred Congregation for the Doctrine of the Faith has reminded all the faithful of Catholic teaching on procured abortion. The congregation now considers it opportune to set forth the Church's teaching on euthanasia.

It is indeed true that, in this sphere of teaching, the recent Popes have explained the principles, and these retain their full force; but the progress of medical science in recent years has brought to the fore new aspects of the question of euthanasia, and these aspects call for further elucidation on the ethical level.

In modern society, in which even the fundamental values of human life are often called into question, cultural change exercises an influence upon the way of looking at suffering and death; moreover, medicine has increased its capacity to cure and to prolong life in particular circumstances, which sometimes give rise to moral problems.

Thus people living in this situation experience no little anxiety about the meaning of advanced old age and death. They also begin to wonder whether they have the right to obtain for themselves or their fellowmen an "easy death," which would shorten suffering and which seems to them more in harmony with human dignity.

A number of episcopal conferences have raised questions on this subject with the Sacred Congregation for the Doctrine of the Faith. The congregation, having sought the opinion of experts on the various aspects of euthanasia, now wishes to respond to the bishops' questions with the present Declaration, in order to help them to give correct teaching to the faithful entrusted to their care, and to offer them elements for reflection that they can present to the civil authorities with regard to this very serious matter.

The considerations set forth in the present document concern in the first place all those who place their faith and hope in Christ, who, through his life, death and resurrection, has given a new meaning to existence and especially to the death of the Christian, as St. Paul says: "If we live, we live to the Lord, and if we die, we die to the Lord" (Rom 14:8; cf. Phil 1:20).

As for those who profess other religions, many will agree with us that faith in God the Creator, Provider and Lord of life— if they share this belief—confers a lofty dignity upon every human person and guarantees respect for him or her.

It is hoped that this Declaration will meet with the approval of many people of good will who, philosophical or ideological differences notwithstanding, have nevertheless a lively awareness of the heights of the human person. These rights have often in fact been proclaimed in recent years through declarations issued by international congresses; and since it is a question here of fundamental rights inherent in every human person, it is obviously wrong to have recourse to arguments from political pluralism or religious freedom in order to deny the universal value of those rights.

I. The Value of Human Life

Human life is the basis of all goods, and is the necessary source and condition of every human activity and of all society. Most people regard life as something sacred and hold that no one may dispose of it at will, but believers see in life something greater, namely a gift of God's love, which they are called upon to preserve and make fruitful. And it is this latter consideration that gives rise to the following consequences:

1. No one can make an attempt on the life of an innocent person without opposing God's love for that person, without violating a fundamental right, and therefore without committing a crime of the utmost gravity.
2. Everyone has the duty to lead his or her life in accordance with God's plan. That life is entrusted to the individual as a good that must bear fruit already here on earth, but that finds its full perfection only in eternal life.
3. Intentionally causing one's own death, or suicide, is therefore equally as wrong as murder; such an action on the part of a person is to be considered as a rejection of God's sovereignty and loving plan. Furthermore, suicide is also often a refusal of love for self, the denial of the natural instinct to live, a flight from the duties of justice and charity owed to one's neighbor, to various communities or to the whole of society—although, as is generally recognized, at times there are psychological factors present that can diminish responsibility or even completely remove it.

However, one must clearly distinguish suicide from that sacrifice of one's life whereby for a higher cause, such as God's glory, the salvation of souls or the service of one's brethren, a person offers his or her own life or puts it in danger (cf. Jn 15:14).

II. Euthanasia

In order that the question of euthanasia can be properly dealt with, it is first necessary to define the words used.

Etymologically speaking, in ancient times euthanasia meant an easy death without severe suffering. Today one no longer thinks of this original meaning of the word, but rather of some intervention of medicine whereby the sufferings of sickness or of the final agony are reduced, sometimes also with the danger of suppressing life prematurely. Ultimately, the word euthanasia is used in a more particular sense to mean "mercy killing," for the purpose of putting an end to extreme suffering, or saving abnormal babies, the mentally ill or the incurably sick from the prolongation, perhaps for many years, of a miserable life, which could impose too heavy a burden on their families or on society.

It is therefore necessary to state clearly in what sense the word is used in the present document.

By euthanasia is understood an action or an omission which of itself or by intention causes death, in order that all suffering may in this way be eliminated. Euthanasia's terms of reference, therefore, are to be found in the intention of the will and in the methods used.

It is necessary to state firmly once more that nothing and no one can in any way permit the killing of an innocent human being, whether a fetus or an embryo, an infant or an adult, an old person, or one suffering from an incurable disease, or a person who is dying. Furthermore, no one is permitted to ask for this act of killing, either for himself or herself or for another person entrusted to his or her care, nor can he or she consent to it, either explicitly or implicitly. Nor can any authority legitimately recommend or permit such an action. For it is a question of the violation of the divine law, an offense against the dignity of the human person, a crime against life, and an attack on humanity.

It may happen that, by reason of prolonged and barely tolerable pain, for deeply personal or other reasons, people may be led to believe that they can legitimately ask for death or obtain it for others. Although in these cases the guilt of the individual may be reduced or completely absent, nevertheless the error of judgment into which the conscience falls, perhaps in good faith, does not change the nature of this act of killing, which will always be in itself something to be rejected.

The pleas of gravely ill people who sometimes ask for death are not to be understood as implying a true desire for euthanasia; in fact it is almost always a case of an anguished plea for help and love. What a sick person needs, besides medical care, is love, the human and supernatural warmth with which the sick person can and ought to be surrounded by all those close to him or her, parents and children, doctors and nurses.

III. The Meaning of Suffering for Christians and the Use of Painkillers

Death does not always come in dramatic circumstances after barely tolerable sufferings. Nor do we have to think only of extreme cases. Numerous testimonies which confirm one another lead one to the conclusion that nature itself has made provision to render more bearable at the moment of death separations that would be terribly painful to a person in full health. Hence it is that a prolonged illness, advanced old age, or a state of loneliness or neglect can bring about psychological conditions that facilitate the acceptance of death.

Nevertheless the fact remains that death, often preceded or accompanied by severe and prolonged suffering, is something which naturally causes people anguish.

Physical suffering is certainly an unavoidable element of the human condition; on the biological level, it constitutes a warning of which no one denies the usefulness; but, since it affects the human psychological makeup, it often exceeds its own biological usefulness and so can become so severe as to cause the desire to remove it at any cost.

According to Christian teaching, however, suffering, especially suffering during the last moments of life, has a special place in God's saving plan; it is in fact a sharing in Christ's passion and a union with the redeeming sacrifice which he offered in obedience to the Father's will. Therefore one must not be surprised if some Christians prefer to moderate their use of painkillers, in order to accept voluntarily at least a part of their sufferings and thus associate themselves in a conscious way with the sufferings of Christ crucified (cf. Mt 27:34).

Nevertheless it would be imprudent to impose an heroic way of acting as a general rule. On the contrary, human and Christian prudence suggests for the majority of sick people the use of medicines capable of alleviating or suppressing pain, even though these may cause as a secondary effect semi-consciousness and reduced lucidity. As for those who are not in a state to express themselves, one can reasonably presume that they wish to take these painkillers, and have them administered according to the doctor's advice.

But the intensive use of painkillers is not without difficulties, because the phenomenon of habituation generally makes it necessary to increase their dosage in order to maintain their efficacy. At this point it is fitting to recall a declaration by Pius XII, which retains its full force, in answer to a group of doctors who had put the question: "Is the suppression of pain and consciousness by the use of narcotics permitted by religion and morality to the doctor and the patient (even at the approach of death and if one foresees that the use of narcotics will shorten life)?"

The Pope said: "If no other means exist, and if, in the given circumstances, this does not prevent the carrying out of other religious and moral duties: Yes." In this case, of course, death is in no way intended or sought, even if the risk of it is reasonably taken; the intention is simply to relieve pain effectively, using for this purpose painkillers available to medicine.

However, painkillers that cause unconsciousness need special consideration. For a person not only has to be able to satisfy his or her moral duties and family obligations; he or she also has to prepare himself or herself with full consciousness for meeting Christ. Thus Pius XII warns: "It is not right to deprive the dying person of consciousness without a serious reason."

IV. Due Proportion in the Use of Remedies

Today it is very important to protect, at the moment of death, both the dignity of the human person and the Christian concept of life against a technological attitude that threatens to become an abuse. Thus, some people speak of a "right to die," which is an expression that does not mean the right to procure death either by one's own hand or by means of someone else, as one pleases, but rather the right to die peacefully with human and Christian dignity. From this point of view, the use of therapeutic means can sometimes pose problems.

In numerous cases, the complexity of the situation can be such as to cause doubts about the way ethical principles should be applied. In the final analysis, it pertains to the conscience either of the sick person, or of those qualified to speak in the sick person's name, or of the doctors, to decide, in the light of moral obligations and of the various aspects of the case.

Everyone has the duty to care for his or her own health or to seek such care from others. Those whose task it is to care for the sick must do so conscientiously and administer the remedies that seem necessary or useful.

However, is it necessary in all circumstances to have recourse to all possible remedies?

In the past, moralists replied that one is never obliged to use "extraordinary" means. This reply, which as a principle still holds good, is perhaps less clear today, by reason of the imprecision of the term and the rapid progress made in the treatment of sickness. Thus some people prefer to speak of "proportionate" and "disproportionate" means.

In any case, it will be possible to make a correct judgment as to the means by studying the type of treatment to be used, its degree of complexity or risk, its cost and the possibilities of using it, and comparing these elements with the result that can be expected, taking into account the state of the sick person and his or her physical and moral resources.

In order to facilitate the application of these general principles, the following clarifications can be added:

— If there are no other sufficient remedies, it is permitted, with the patient's consent, to have recourse to the means provided by the most advanced medical techniques, even if these means are still at the experimental stage and are not without a certain risk. By accepting them, the patient can even show generosity in the service of humanity.

— It is also permitted, with the patient's consent, to interrupt these means, where the results fall short of expectations. But for such a decision to be made, account will have to be taken of the reasonable wishes of the patient's family, as also of the advice of the doctors who are specially competent in the matter. The latter may in particular judge that the investment in instruments and personnel is disproportionate to the results foreseen; they may also judge that the techniques applied impose on the patient strain or suffering out of proportion with the benefits which he or she may gain from such techniques.

— It is also permissible to make do with the normal means that medicine can offer. Therefore one cannot impose on anyone the obligation to have recourse to a technique which is already in use but which carries a risk or is burdensome. Such a refusal is not the equivalent of suicide; on the contrary, it should be considered as an acceptance of the human condition, or a wish to avoid the application of a medical procedure disproportionate to the results that can be expected, or a desire not to impose excessive expense on the family or the community.

— When inevitable death is imminent in spite of the means used, it is permitted in conscience to take the decision to refuse forms of treatment that would only secure a precarious and burdensome prolongation of life, so long as the normal care due to the sick person in similar cases is not interrupted. In such circumstances the doctor has no reason to reproach himself with failing to help the person in danger.

Conclusion

The norms contained in the present Declaration are inspired by a profound desire to serve people in accordance with the plan of the Creator. Life is a gift of God, and on the other hand death is unavoidable; it is necessary therefore that we, without in any way hastening the hour of death, should be able to accept it with full responsibility and dignity. It is true that death marks the end of our earthly existence, but at the same time it opens the door to immortal life. Therefore all must prepare themselves for this event in the light of human values, and Christians even more so in the light of faith.

As for those who work in the medical profession, they ought to neglect no means of making all their skill available to the sick and the dying; but they should also remember how much more necessary it is to provide them with the comfort of boundless kindness and heartfelt charity. Such service to people is also service to Christ the Lord, who said: "As you did it to one of the least of these my brethren, you did it to me"(Mt 25:40).

At the audience granted to the undersigned prefect, His Holiness Pope John Paul II approved this Declaration, adopted at the ordinary meeting of the Sacred Congregation for the Doctrine of the Faith, and ordered its publication.

Rome, the Sacred Congregation for the Doctrine of the Faith, 5 May 1980.

Franjo Card. Seper
Prefect
Jerome Hamer, O.P.
Tit. Archibishop of Lorium, Secretary

Notes

Introduction

1. A fine analysis of the terminological complexity of the definition of "euthanasia" is in Tom L. Beauchamp and Arnold I. Davidson, "The Definition of Euthanasia," *The Journal of Medicine and Philosophy* 4 (September 1979): 294–312. Also helpful for sorting through some of the philosophical issues is the President's Commission for the Study of Ethical Problems in Medicine and Biomedical and Behavioral Research, *Deciding to Forego Life-Sustaining Treatment* (Washington: U.S. Government Printing Office, 1983), see especially Chapter Two, pp. 43–90.

Chapter 1
Determining Death

1. Robert M. Veatch, *Death, Dying, and the Biological Revolution: Our Last Quest for Responsibility* (New Haven: Yale University Press, 1976), p. 33. For a similar position, see Paul Ramsey, "On Updating Death" in Donald R. Cutler, ed., *Updating Life and Death* (Boston: Beacon Press, 1968), pp. 31–54, esp. p. 52.

2. Dallas M. High, "Death, Definition and Determination of: Conceptual Foundations: III: Philosophical and Theological Foundations," in *Encyclopedia of Bioethics I* (New York: The Free Press, 1978), pp. 301–307.

3. Veatch, *Death, Dying, and the Biological Revolution, pp. 29–42.*

4. *On the Theology of Death,* Vol. 2: *Quaestiones Disputatae* (New York: Herder and Herder, 1961), pp. 16–26.

5. *AAS* 45 (November 24, 1957): 1027–1033, at p. 1033. Translation from "The Prolongation of Life," *The Pope Speaks* 4 (Spring 1958): 393–398, at p. 397.

6. "Theological Considerations Concerning the Moment of Death," *Theological Investigations,* Vol, XI: *Confrontations,* trans. by David Bourke (New York: Seabury Press, 1974), pp. 311–312. In this article Rahner goes on to endorse the concept of whole brain death as being consistent with his theological view, though he recognizes that the biologist and medical scientists have to work out the precise criteria for deciding when this takes place.

7. Culver and Gert, *Philosophy in Medicine* (New York: Oxford University Press, 1982), p. 181.

8. *The Dignity of Life: Moral Values in a Changing Society* (Huntington: Our Sunday Visitor, Inc., 1976), p. 202. McFadden's context suggests he is using the ambiguous expression "brain death" to mean "whole brain death."

9. *Medical Ethics* (Notre Dame: Fides Publishers, Inc., 1973), p. 136. Häring's context suggests he is using the ambiguous expression "brain death" to mean "whole brain death."

10. "On Updating Death," in Cutler, ed., *Updating Life and Death,* pp. 31–54, quotation at p. 52. See also Ramsey, *The Patient as Person: Explorations in Medical Ethics* (New Haven: Yale University Press, 1970), pp. 101–112.

11. President's Commission, *Defining Death: Medical, Legal and Ethical Issues in the Determination of Death,* Morris B. Abram, Chairman (Washington: U.S. Government Printing Office, 1981), p. 33. Evidence of the commission's specific adoption of this whole brain concept of death as the basis for recommending statutory standards is on p. 36.

12. "A Definition of Irreversible Coma," a report of the Ad Hoc Committee of the Harvard Medical School, *Journal of the American Medical Association* 205 (August 1968): 337–340.

13. Adrienne Van Till—d'Aulnis de Bourouill, "Diagnosis of Death in Comatose Patients under Resuscitation: A Critical Review of the Harvard Report," *American Journal of Law and Medicine* 2 (Summer 1976): 1–40. Cited by Douglas N. Walton, *Brain Death: Ethical Considerations* (West Lafayette: Purdue University Press, 1980), pp. 23–25. Also cited by U.S. Bishops' Committee for Pro-Life Activities, "Resource Paper on Definition of Death Legislation," *Origins* 13 (May 26, 1983), p. 44.

14. Paul A. Byrne, Sean O'Reilly and Paul M. Quay, "Brain Death: An Opposing Viewpoint," *Journal of the American Medical Association* 242 (Nov. 2, 1979), pp. 1985–1990; see also Paul A. Byrne, "Response," in Donald G. McCarthy and Albert S. Moraczewski, eds., *Moral Responsibility in Prolonging Life Decisions* (St. Louis: Pope John Center, 1981), pp. 53–57. A summary of this viewpoint is in the U.S. Bishops' Com-

mittee for Pro-Life Activities, "Resource Paper on Definition of Death Legislation," *Origins* 13 (May 26, 1983), 42–44.

15. Dennis J. Horan, "Determination of Death: A Medical-Legal Consensus," in Donald G. McCarthy and Albert S. Moraczewski, eds., *Moral Responsibility in Prolonging Life Decisions* (St. Louis: Pope John Center, 1981), pp. 58–70, at p. 67.

16. As reported in Walton, *Brain Death*, p. 15. Robert M. Veatch cites a similar study with the same results conducted by a committee of the Institute of Society, Ethics and the Life Sciences. See Veatch, *Death, Dying, and the Biological Revolution*, p. 48. See also the report by Frank J. Veith, *et al.,* "Brain Death: I. A Status Report of Medical and Ethical Considerations," *Journal of the American Medical Association* 238 (October 10, 1977): 1651–1655, at p. 1652.

17. Other studies have also been done to establish criteria for determining whole brain death. Some place greater emphasis on clinical judgment without recourse to an EEG reading; others are even more conservative than the Harvard criteria and require supplementary techniques to confirm the EEG readings. Some of these other techniques are angiographic techniques, metabolic techniques, determination of oxygen consumption, determination of lactic acid in the spinal fluid. Walton, *Brain Death*, pp. 15–29.

18. President's Commission, *Defining Death*, Appendix F, "Guidelines for the Determination of Death," pp. 159–166.

19. Veatch, *Death, Dying, and the Biological Revolution*, pp. 42–50.

20. As recorded in Albert S. Moraczewski and J. Stuart Showalter, *Determination of Death: Theological, Medical, Ethical, and Legal Issues* (St. Louis: Catholic Health Association, 1982), p. 21.

21. President's Commission, *Defining Death*, p. 127.

22. Frank Veith, *et al.,* "Brain Death: II. A Status Report of Legal Considerations," *Journal of the American Medical Association* 238 (October 17, 1977): 1744–1748, at p. 1747.

23. President's Commission, *Defining Death*, p. 73.

24. *Ibid.,* pp. 128–129.

25. *Ibid.,* p. 124.

26. See the conclusions of the Pro-Life Committee's "Resource Paper," in *Origins* 13 (May 26, 1983): 27.

27. "Defining Death" *Origins* 11 (August 13, 1981): 156–157.

28. "Supporting a Determination of Death Bill," *Origins* 11 (March 4, 1982): 599–600.

29. Moraczewski and Showalter, *Determination of Death*, p. 28.

Chapter 2
The Moral Issues

1. "The Sanctity of Life," in *Updating Life and Death,* edited by Donald R. Cutler (Boston: Beacon Press, 1969), p. 184.

2. *Ibid.,* pp. 184–185.

3. *The Contributions of Theology to Medical Ethics* (Milwaukee: Marquette University Theology Department, 1975), p. 56.

4. *The Right to Life* (New York: Holt, Rinehart and Winston, 1963), p. 12. For another Catholic view which situates sanctity of life within a religious understanding of the human person, see *Handbook on Critical Life Issues,* edited by Donald G. McCarthy and Edward J. Bayer (St. Louis: Pope John Center, 1982), esp. pp. 18, 40–44.

5. "The Morality of Abortion," in *Life or Death: Ethics and Options,* edited by Daniel H. Labby (Seattle: University of Washington Press, 1968), p. 71. Charles E. Curran objects to Ramsey's notion of "alien dignity" on the basis that it minimizes other human ways of valuing life which are based on "criteria inherent in individual human life." *Politics, Medicine, and Christian Ethics: A Dialogue with Paul Ramsey* (Philadelphia: Fortress Press, 1973), p. 121.

6. *The Moral Choice* (Garden City: Doubleday & Company, Inc., 1978), p. 83.

7. *Ibid.,* p. 72.

8. "The Sanctity of Life," *Life or Death: Ethics and Options,* pp. 18–19.

9. *Ibid.,* p. 3. Other factors which he sees operating to raise the question of the sanctity of life are the increased confidence of biomedical science, the increased capacity for contrived intervention into social behavior through electronic surveillance and the use of drugs, the unprecedented experience of the Nazi destruction of human life, and the dropping of two atomic bombs. See pp. 4–5.

10. *Ibid.,* p. 12.

11. For some of these objections, see Callahan, "Sanctity of Life," *Updating Life and Death,* pp. 191–192; cf. Callahan, *Abortion: Law, Choice and Morality* (New York: The Macmillan Company, 1970), p. 314. The chapter "Sanctity of Life" in this book is substantially the reproduction of his earlier essay, though it does include some revision based on responses Callahan received to his earlier essay.

12. "Sanctity of Life," *Life or Death: Ethics and Options,* pp. 36–37.

13. *Ibid.,* pp. 14–15.

14. *The Right to Life,* p. 14.

15. Gustafson, *The Contributions of Theology to Medical Ethics,* p. 57.

16. *Ibid.,* pp. 62–63.

17. St Louis: The Catholic Health Association, 1983.

18. *Ibid.,* p. 83.

19. "The Sanctity of Life," *Updating Life and Death,* pp. 196–220; cf. *Abortion,* pp. 323–346; quotation from "The Sanctity of Life," *Updating Life and Death,* p. 200; cf. *Abortion,* p. 326.

20. For Callahan's examination of the rule systems bearing on the sanctity of life principle which bring out the latent content in the principle, see "The Sanctity of Life," *Updating Life and Death,* pp. 202–207; cf. *Abortion,* pp. 328–333.

21. *The Right to Life,* p. 12.

22. *Free and Faithful in Christ,* Vol. 3: *Light to the World* (New York: Crossroad Publishing Co., 1981), p. 5.

23. "The Morality of Abortion," *Life or Death: Ethics and Options,* p. 73. For the related theme in Karl Barth, see *Church Dogmatics* III/4 (Edinburgh: T. and T. Clark, 1961), p. 335.

24. *Morals in Medicine* (Westminster: The Newman Press, 1956), p. 52.

25. New York: Alba House, 1976.

26. *Ibid.,* pp. 42–43.

27. New York: The Edwin Mellen Press, 1979.

28. *Ibid.,* pp. 436–447.

29. Milwaukee: Marquette University Theology Department, 1975, p. 25.

30. *Ibid.,* pp. 62, 76, 80.

31. *Medical Ethics* (Notre Dame: Fides Publishers, Inc., 1973), p. 149. Häring refers in a footnote to R. Kautuzky, "Der Arzt," p. 138. Presumably the quoted material within this excerpt is from Kautuzky.

32. *Catholic Perspectives: The Right To Die* (Chicago: Thomas More Press, 1980), pp. 91–92; cf. *Morality and Its Beyond* (Mystic, CT: Twenty-Third Publications, 1984), pp. 242–243.

33. *Morality and Its Beyond,* p. 238; cf. *Catholic Perspectives,* pp. 68–69; also cf. *What a Modern Catholic Believes About the Right to Life* (Chicago: Thomas More Press, 1973), p. 63.

34. *Death by Choice,* Updated and Expanded Edition (Garden City: Doubleday & Company, Inc., 1984), p. 119.

35. "Zur Problematik Allgemein verbindlicher ethischer Grundsatze," *Theologie und Philosophie* 45 (1970), pp. 13–14. Translation

from Richard A. McCormick, "The New Medicine and Morality," *Theology Digest* 21 (Winter 1973): 315.

36. "Active and Passive Euthanasia," *The New England Journal of Medicine* 292 (January 9, 1975): 78–80. This article is about one-third the length of his fuller treatment of this topic which appeared as "Euthanasia, Killing, and Letting Die" in *Ethical Issues Relating to Life and Death,* edited by John Ladd (New York: Oxford University Press, 1979), pp. 146–163.

37. *Life and Death with Liberty and Justice* (Notre Dame: University of Notre Dame Press, 1979), pp. 414–415. See also the defense of the moral difference between killing and letting die on the basis of "intention" in Joseph M. Boyle, Jr. "On Killing and Letting Die," *The New Scholasticism* 51 (Autumn 1977): 433–452.

38. For an analysis of the principle of double effect and a review of its recent evaluation, see Richard A. McCormick, "The Principle of Double Effect," *How Brave a New World?* (Garden City: Doubleday & Company, Inc., 1981), pp. 413–429; Charles E. Curran, "The Principle of Double Effect," *Ongoing Revision: Studies in Moral Theology* (Notre Dame: Fides Publishers, Inc., 1975), pp. 173–209; also David F. Kelly, *The Emergence of Roman Catholic Medical Ethics in North America* (New York: The Edwin Mellen Press, 1979), pp. 244–274.

39. For a discussion of the direct and indirect distinction on the formulation of moral norms, see Bruno Schüller, "Direct Killing/Indirect Killing," in *Readings in Moral Theology No. 1: Moral Norms and Catholic Tradition,* edited by Charles E. Curran and Richard A. McCormick (Ramsey: Paulist Press, 1979), pp. 138–157.

40. Ramsey: Paulist Press, 1982, pp. 61–81.

41. The method of "proportionalism" which underlies this re-evaluation of the conditions of the principle of double effect has come under criticism. For example, Cardinal Ratzinger has been critical of efforts which make "proportionalism" the exclusive method for arriving at a moral judgment. He wants to preserve the "intrinsic" morality of an action. See his "Dissent and Proportionalism in Moral Theology," *Origins* 13 (March 15, 1984): 666–669. Germain Grisez has also criticized proportionalism as being incompatible with Christian faith. See his *The Way of the Lord Jesus,* Vol. 1: *Christian Moral Principles* (Chicago: Franciscan Herald Press, 1983), pp. 141–171. Paul E. McKeever has reviewed proportionalism and identified some of its major points of controversy as well as showing ways proportionalism responds to each objection. See his "Proportionalism As a Methodology," in *Human Sexuality and Personhood* (St. Louis: Pope John Center, 1981), pp. 211–222.

Philip S. Keane has offered a thorough review of proportionalism by taking a critical look at its difficulties as well as suggesting its areas which need further study. See his "The Objective Moral Order: Reflections on Recent Research," *Theological Studies* 43 (June 1982): 260–278.

42. President's Commission, *Deciding to Forego Life-Sustaining Treatment* (Washington: U.S. Government Printing Office, 1983), p. 82. The full discussion of this distinction is found on pp. 77–82.

43. Robert M. Veatch, *Death, Dying, and the Biological Revolution* (New Haven: Yale University Press, 1976), pp. 85–86.

44. *Ibid.*, pp. 82–83.

45. *Ibid.*, pp. 84–85.

46. *Ibid.*, pp. 86–90.

47. *Ibid.*, pp. 90–93. For another careful analysis of the inadequacy of the "cause of death" as sufficient to justify the moral difference between omission and commission, see President's Commission, *Deciding to Forego Life-Sustaining Treatment,* pp. 68–70.

48. *Death by Choice,* Updated and Expanded Edition, pp. 98–101. The four ways in which omission and commission differ in Maguire's study are (1) their effects, (2) their deliberateness, (3) the specificity of agency, and (4) their variety of forms.

49. "Are Killing and Letting Die Morally Different in Medical Contexts?" *The Journal of Medicine and Philosophy* 4 (September 1979): 269–293. Menzel considers ten ways to make a moral difference between killing and letting die in medical contexts: (1) the imperative "do no harm"; (2) mistaken prognosis of terminal illness; (3) closure of others' options; (4) the difficulty and dischargeability of duties; (5) dampening progress in medicine and health care; (6) escaping the burdens of the weak and dependent; (7) differential benefits to outweigh abuses; (8) the requirement of informed consent; (9) using one life to preserve others (competing lives); (10) domination.

50. *Death, Dying, and the Biological Revolution,* p. 93.

51. Gilbert Meilaender, "The Distinction Between Killing and Allowing To Die," *Theological Studies* 37 (September 1976): 467–470. The position of Ramsey to which Meilaender refers is found in Paul Ramsey, *The Patient as Person* (New Haven: Yale University Press, 1970), pp. 146–157. For another position which relies on religious convictions to sustain the distinction, see Stanley Hauerwas with Richard Bondi and David B. Burrell, "Memory, Community and the Reasons for Living: Reflections on Suicide and Euthanasia," *Truthfulness and Tragedy* (Notre Dame: University of Notre Dame Press, 1977), pp. 101–115.

52. Tom L. Beauchamp, "A Reply to Rachels on Active and Passive Euthanasia," in Tom L. Beauchamp and Seymour Perlin, eds., *Ethical Issues in Death and Dying* (Englewood Cliffs: Prentice-Hall, Inc., 1978), p. 253.

53. James F. Childress, "To Kill or Let Die," in Elsie L. Bandman and Bertram Bandman, eds., *Bioethics and Human Rights: A Reader for Health Professionals* (Boston: Little, Brown and Company, 1978), p. 128.

54. James J. McCartney, "The Development of the Doctrine of Ordinary and Extraordinary Means of Preserving Life in Catholic Moral Theology Before the Karen Quinlan Case," *Linacre Quarterly* 47 (August 1980): 216.

55. *Medico-Moral Problems* (St. Louis: The Catholic Hospital Association, 1958), p. 129.

56. *AAS* 49 (1957), pp. 1031–1032.

57. Kelly, *Medico-Moral Problems,* p. 134.

58. *The Patient as Person,* pp. 120–124.

59. *Medico-Moral Problems,* p. 130. See also his earlier and more extensive treatment of this issue in his article "The Duty of Using Artificial Means of Preserving Life," *Theological Studies* 11 (June 1950): 203–220.

60. *Medical Ethics* (Chicago: Loyola University Press, 1956), p. 80.

61. *The Dignity of Life* (Huntington: Our Sunday Visitor, Inc., 1976), pp. 152–156; also, *Challenge to Morality* (Huntington: Our Sunday Visitor, Inc. 1978), pp. 192–193.

62. Committee for Pro-Life Activities (Washington: National Conference of Catholic Bishops, 1984).

63. President's Commission, *Deciding to Forego Life-Sustaining Treatment,* p. 190.

64. Sidney H. Wanzer, *et al.,* "The Physician's Responsibility Toward Hopelessly Ill Patients," *New England Journal of Medicine* 310 (April 12, 1984): 958.

65. *Ibid.*

66. "Must Patients Always Be Given Food and Water?" *The Hastings Center Report* 13 (October 1983): 17–21.

67. For a discussion of this issue as it pertains to newborns, see Carson Strong, "Can Fluids and Electrolytes Be 'Extraordinary' Treatment?" *Journal of Medical Ethics* 7 (1981): 83–85.

68. For a discussion of this issue as it pertains to the elderly, see David T. Watts and Christine K. Cassell, "Extraordinary Nutritional Support: A Case Study and Ethical Analysis," *Journal of the American Geriatrics Society* 32 (March 1984): 237–243.

69. Childress and Lynn, "Must Patients Always Be Given Food and Water?" *The Hastings Center Report,* p. 21.

70. Callahan, "On Feeding the Dying," *The Hastings Center Report* 13 (October 1983): 22.

71. Gilbert Meilaender, "On Removing Food and Water: Against the Stream," *The Hastings Center Report* 14 (December 1984): 11–12.

72. Callahan, "On Feeding the Dying," *The Hastings Center Report* 13 (October 1983): 22.

73. *Ibid.,* cf. Meilaender, "On Removing Food and Water," *The Hastings Center Report,* p. 11.

74. *Ibid.,* p. 13.

75. McCormick, "Caring or Starving? The Case of Claire Conroy," *America* 152 (April 6, 1985): 269–273; see especially pp. 272–273.

76. *Ibid.,* p. 273.

77. President's Commission, *Deciding to Forego Life-Sustaining Treatment,* p. 89. For the commission's discussion of this issue, see pp. 82–89.

78. Albert R. Jonsen, "What Is Extraordinary Life Support?—Medical Staff Conference, University of California, San Francisco," *The Western Journal of Medicine* 141 (September 1984): 361–362.

79. "Prolonging Life: The Duty and Its Limits," in *Moral Responsibility in Prolonging Life Decisions,* edited by Donald G. McCarthy and Albert S. Moraczewski (St. Louis: Pope John Center, 1981), p. 129; cf. "Prolonging Life: The Duty and Its Limits," *Linacre Quarterly* 47 (May 1980): 155.

80. Connery's most vigorous defense of "burden" as the decisive factor against "quality-of-life" considerations is in "The Clarence Herbert Case: Was Withdrawal of Treatment Justified?" *Hospital Progress* 65 (February 1984): 32–35, 70.

81. "Moral Notes," *Theological Studies* 36 (March 1975): 121; cf. "Moral Notes," *Theological Studies* 42 (March 1981): 104–105.

82. This theme is developed in his "The Quality of Life, The Sanctity of Life," *How Brave a New World?* pp. 383–401.

83. Richard A. McCormick, "To Save or Let Die: The Dilemma of Modern Medicine," *How Brave a New World?* p. 349. This article was also published simultaneously in *America* 131 (July 13, 1974): 6–10, and *JAMA* 229 (July 8, 1974): 172–176. For some responses to this position, see *America* 131 (October 5, 1974): 169–173.

84. *Ethics at the Edges of Life* (New Haven: Yale University Press, 1978), p. 155.

85. *Death, Dying, and the Biological Revolution,* p. 112.

Chapter 3
The Moral Positions

1. For a very fine discussion of the various forms of teleological and deontological theories, see *Principles of Biomedical Ethics,* by Tom L. Beauchamp and James F. Childress, Second Edition (New York: Oxford University Press, 1983), pp. 19–58.

2. Ramsey: Paulist Press, 1982, pp. 58–89.

3. Philadelphia: Westminster Press, 1966.

4. *Ibid.,* p. 30.

5. Boston: Beacon Press, 1954.

6. *Moral Responsibility* (Philadelphia: Westminster Press, 1967), p. 151.

7. *Morals and Medicine,* pp. 192–193, 208–209; cf. *Moral Responsibility,* p. 151, and "Ethics and Euthanasia," *American Journal of Nursing* 73 (1973), pp. 670–675. This article also appears in *To Live and To Die,* edited by Robert H. Williams (New York: Springer-Verlag, 1973), pp. 113–122. All page references to this article are taken from Williams. On Fletcher's understanding of God's role in medicine, see especially pp. 115–116.

8. *Moral Responsibility,* p. 151.

9. "Ethics and Euthanasia," p. 115.

10. *Ibid.*

11. *Ibid.,* p. 121; cf. *Moral Responsibility,* p. 150.

12. *Moral Responsibility,* pp. 154–155.

13. "Ethics and Euthanasia," p. 113.

14. *Ibid.*

15. *Morals and Medicine,* pp. 207–208.

16. "Ethics and Euthanasia," pp. 119–120.

17. "Voluntary Beneficent Euthanasia," in *Beneficent Euthanasia,* edited by Marvin Kohl (Buffalo: Prometheus Books, 1975), p. 135.

18. Atlantic Highlands, N.J.: Humanities Press, 1974.

19. *Ibid.,* p. 30. His examination of sanctity-of-life and its satellite expressions is on pp. 1–23.

20. *Ibid.,* p. 95.

21. *Ibid.,* p. 106.

22. *Ibid.,* pp. 95–96.

23. *Ibid.,* p. 133; for his argument from justice, see pp. 135–137; cf. *The Morality of Killing,* p. 106.

24. "Voluntary Beneficent Euthanasia," p. 136.

25. See especially his essay, co-authored with Richard Bondi, "Memory, Community and the Reasons for Living: Reflections on Suicide and Euthanasia," in *Truthfulness and Tragedy,* with Richard Bondi and David B. Burrell (Notre Dame: University of Notre Dame Press, 1977), pp. 101–115.

26. *Ibid.,* p. 115.

27. This is the theme of his article, "Must a Patient Be a Person to Be a Patient? Or, My Uncle Charlie Is Not Much of a Person But He Is Still My Uncle Charlie," in *Truthfulness and Tragedy,* pp. 127–131.

28. Hauerwas explores this issue as it pertains to caring for retarded children. See his "Suffering, Medical Ethics and the Retarded Child," *Truthfulness and Tragedy,* pp. 164–168.

29. The first edition appeared in 1974. Doubleday and Company, Inc. has now published an Image Book, paperback version of his "updated and expanded" edition. The references to Maguire will be from this most recent edition.

30. Garden City: Doubleday & Company, Inc., 1978.

31. *Death by Choice,* Updated and Expanded Edition (1984), p. 11.

32. *Ibid.,* p. 119.

33. He first developed this position in "Freedom to Die," in *New Theology No. 10,* edited by Martin E. Marty and Dean G. Peerman (New York: The Macmillan Company, 1973), pp. 194–195; cf. *Death by Choice,* Updated and Expanded Edition (1984), p. 83.

34. *Ibid.,* p. 107.

35. "Death and the Moral Domain," *St. Luke's Journal of Theology* 20 (June 1977), p. 216.

36. "Respect for Life: Theoretical and Practical Implications," *Issues in Sexual and Medical Ethics* (Notre Dame: University of Notre Dame Press, 1978), pp. 198–199; cf. "The Fifth Commandment: Thou Shalt Not Kill," *Ongoing Revision: Studies in Moral Theology* (Notre Dame: Fides Publishers, Inc., 1975), p. 145.

37. "The Fifth Commandment," *Ongoing Revision,* pp. 145–146; cf. "Respect for Life," *Issues,* p. 200.

38. *Politics, Medicine and Christian Ethics: A Dialogue with Paul Ramsey* (Philadelphia: Fortress Press, 1973), p. 161.

39. "The Fifth Commandment," *Ongoing Revision,* p. 151.

40. *Ibid.,* p. 152.

41. *Ibid.,* pp. 150–152; cf. "The Principle of Double Effect," *Ongoing Revision,* pp. 190–209, especially pp. 202–205.

42. "The Fifth Commandment," *Ongoing Revision,* p. 160; cf. *Politics, Medicine and Christian Ethics,* pp. 161–162.

43. *Ibid.*

44. "The New Medicine and Morality," *Theology Digest* 21 (Winter 1973): 316. He develops this premoral evil/proportionate reason thought-pattern more extensively in his *Ambiguity in Moral Choice* (Milwaukee: Marquette University Press, 1973).

45. "The New Medicine and Morality," p. 316.

46. *Ibid.,* p. 317.

47. *Ibid.*

48. *Ibid.,* p. 318.

49. *Ibid.;* see also, "Moral Notes," *Theological Studies* 34 (March 1973): 72–74.

50. A brief survey of points of criticism raised against proportionalism as a method can be found in Paul E. McKeever, "Proportionalism as a Methodology in Catholic Moral Theology," *Human Sexuality and Personhood* (St. Louis: Pope John Center, 1981), pp. 211–222. For a more thorough review of proportionalism, its critical features and its areas needing further development, see Philip S. Keane, "The Objective Moral Order: Reflections on Recent Research," *Theological Studies* 43 (June 1982): 260–278. For an assessment of proportionalism which finds it ultimately unacceptable as a theory of moral judgment, see Germain Grisez, *The Way of the Lord Jesus,* Vol. 1: *Christian Moral Principles* (Chicago: Franciscan Herald Press, 1983), pp. 141–171. An extensive challenge to this method along with a response from Richard McCormick can be found in Richard McCormick and Paul Ramsey, editors, *Doing Evil to Achieve Good* (Chicago: Loyola University Press, 1978).

51. Grisez, *Christian Moral Principles,* pp. 141–171; see especially pp. 142–145, 147–148, 160.

52. Cardinal Joseph Ratzinger, "Dissent and Proportionalism in Moral Theology," *Origins* 13 (March 15, 1984): 666–669.

53. New Haven: Yale University Press, 1970.

54. *Ibid.,* p. xiii.

55. *Ethics at the Edges of Life,* p. 147.

56. *The Patient as Person,* p. 153, see also p. 156.

57. *Ethics at the Edges of Life,* p. 192.

58. *The Patient as Person,* p. 151; see also pp. 159; 162.

59. *Ibid.,* pp. 162–163. The example of infants with Lesch-Nyhan syndrome is introduced in his treatment of this case in *Ethics at the Edges of Life,* pp. 214–215.

60. *The Patient as Person,* pp. 161–162.

61. On Ramsey's confidence that these exceptions will not weaken the general principle to protect life, see *The Patient as Person,* pp. 160–164, and *Ethics at the Edges of Life,* pp. 219–227.

62. *AAS* 72 (1980), pp. 542–552. Also available from USCC publications office, Washington, D.C. Translated as "Vatican Declaration on Euthanasia," *Origins* 10 (August 14, 1980): 154–157. The excerpts used here are from this translation.

63. Notre Dame: University of Notre Dame Press, 1979.

64. Chicago: Franciscan Herald Press, 1977.

65. *Life and Death with Liberty and Justice,* pp. 379–380. For May's treatment of anthropology, see *Human Existence, Medicine and Ethics,* p. 142; for a more extensive treatment, see his essay in *Catholic Perspectives: The Right to Die,* by William E. May and Richard Westley (Chicago: Thomas More Press, 1980), pp. 26–30.

66. *Life and Death with Liberty and Justice,* pp. 359–360. In *Abortion: The Myths, the Realities, and the Arguments* (New York: Corpus Books, 1970), pp. 312–313, Grisez gives this listing of the basic human goods: life itself, activities engaged in for their own sake; experiences sought for their own sake; knowledge pursued for its own sake; interior integrity; genuineness (conformity between one's inner self and his outward behavior), justice and friendship, worship and holiness. William E. May gives this list: life, health, freedom, dignity, justice, peace, knowledge, friendship. See his essay in *Catholic Perspectives,* p. 30.

67. *Life and Death with Liberty and Justice,* p. 364.

68. *Ibid.,* pp. 368–371.

69. *Ibid.,* p. 368.

70. *Human Existence, Medicine and Ethics,* pp. 141–142.

71. *Life and Death with Liberty and Justice,* pp. 393, 394, 412–422; in May, *Human Existence, Medicine and Ethics,* pp. 144–150.

72. "Ethics and Human Identity: The Challenge of the New Biology," *Horizons* 3 (Spring 1976), pp. 36–37.

73. "An Alternative to the Ethic of Euthanasia," in *To Live and To Die,* edited by Robert H. Williams (New York: Springer-Verlag, 1974), p. 102; cf. "Beneficent Euthanasia and Benemortasia: Alternative Views of Mercy," in *Beneficent Euthanasia,* edited by Marvin Kohl (Buffalo: Prometheus Books, 1975), p. 127.

74. *On Human Care: An Introduction to Ethics* (Nashville: Abingdon Press, 1977).

75. *Ibid.,* p. 86.

76. *Ibid.,* pp. 83–84.

77. *Ibid.*, pp. 81–90.
78. "An Alternative to the Ethic of Euthanasia," p. 103; cf. *On Human Care*, p. 82.
79. *On Human Care*, p. 89.
80. "An Alternative to the Ethic of Euthanasia," p. 104.
81. *On Human Care*, p. 85; cf. "Beneficent Euthanasia," and Benemortasia: Alternative Views of Mercy," p. 126.
82. "An Alternative to the Ethic of Euthanasia," pp. 105–106; cf. *On Human Care*, p. 84.
83. "An Alternative to the Ethic of Euthanasia," pp. 110–111; cf. "Beneficent Euthanasia and Benemortasia: Alternative Views of Mercy," p. 127.
84. *A Treasury of Albert Schweitzer*, edited by Thomas Kiernan (New York: The Citadel Press, 1965), p. 19.
85. *Ibid.*, p. 214.
86. *Ibid.*, p. 215.
87. *Time* 78 (November 3, 1961), p. 60.
88. As quoted in Richard A. McCormick and John J. Paris, "Living-Will Legislation Reconsidered," *America* 145 (September 5, 1981): 88.
89. *Ibid.*
90. *Ibid.*
91. Bruno Schüller, "Direct Killing/Indirect Killing" in *Readings in Moral Theology No. 1: Moral Norms and Catholic Tradition*, edited by Charles E. Curran and Richard A. McCormick (Ramsey: Paulist Press, 1979), pp. 138–157; see especially pp. 142–144.

Chapter 4
Caring for the Dying

1. *Medico-Moral Problems* (St. Louis: The Catholic Hospital Association, 1958), p. 136.
2. *Death, Dying, and the Biological Revolution* (New Haven: Yale University Press, 1976), p. 120.
3. Albert R. Jonsen, Mark Siegler and William J. Winslade, *Clinical Ethics* (New York: Macmillan Publishing Co., Inc., 1982), pp. 57–58.
4. *Making Health Care Decisions*, Vol. 1: *Report: The Ethical and Legal Implications of Informed Consent in the Patient-Practitioner Rela-*

tionship (Washington, D.C.: U.S. Government Printing Office, 1982), p. 57.

5. *Ibid.,* pp. 60–61.

6. *Ibid.,* p. 171.

7. *Ibid.,* p. 62.

8. New York: Oxford University Press, 1982.

9. *Priorities in Biomedical Ethics* (Philadelphia: The Westminster Press, 1981), pp. 46–47. For a thorough discussion of the conditions which justify paternalistic intervention, see *Who Should Decide?* pp. 102–113.

10. *Ethics at the Edges of Life* (New Haven: Yale University Press, 1978), p. 156.

11. *Ibid.,* pp. 157, 187–188.

12. *Making Health Care Decisions,* Vol. 1: *Report,* pp. 180–181. Also, *Deciding To Forego Life-Sustaining Treatment* (Washington: U.S. Government Printing Office, 1983), p. 136.

13. For samples of some of the "natural death" statutes and proposals, see President's Commission, *Deciding to Forego Life-Sustaining Treatment,* Appendix D, pp. 310–387. For a brief review of what "natural death acts" are and some of the issues they have raised, see Nina Novak, "'Natural Death Acts' Let Patients Refuse Treatment," *Hospitals* 58 (August 1, 1984): 71–73.

14. For an assessment of the use of living wills in the clinical setting, see Stuart J. Eisendrath and Albert R. Jonsen, "The Living Will: Help or Hindrance?" *Journal of the American Medical Association* 249 (April 15, 1983): 2054–2058.

15. For an example of a Catholic Conference opposition to living-will legislation, see "Living-Will Legislation Opposed: Massachusetts," *Origins* 9 (March 20, 1980): 650–651. Karen Lebacqz, "Commentary 'On Natural Death,'" *The Hastings Center Report* 7 (April 1977): 14. Dennis J. Horan, "Right-to-Die Laws: Creating, Not Clarifying Problems," *Hospital Progress* 59 (June 1978): 62–65, 78; also, "Euthanasia, The Right to Life and Termination of Medical Treatment: Legal Issues," in *Moral Responsibility in Prolonging Life Decisions,* pp. 147–179.

16. President's Commission, *Deciding to Forego Life-Sustaining Treatment,* p. 145.

17. Richard A. McCormick and Andre E. Hellegers, "Legislation and the Living Will," *America* 141 (March 12, 1977): 210–213. This article is now available in the Georgetown University Press paperback edi-

tion of the expanded version of McCormick, *How Brave a New World?* pp. 412–422.

18. Richard A. McCormick and John J. Paris, "Living-Will Legislation, Reconsidered," *America* 145 (September 5, 1981): 86–89. This article is now available in the Georgetown University Press paperback edition of the expanded version of McCormick, *How Brave a New World?* pp. 423–430.

19. *Ibid.,* p. 87.

20. An excellent brief article that explains the durable power of attorney for health care as it applies to the state of California can be found in Michael Gilfix and Thomas A. Raffin, "Withholding or Withdrawing Extraordinary Life Support: Optimizing Rights and Limiting Liability," *The Western Journal of Medicine* 141 (September 1984): 387–394. A succinct evaluation of the California law with its limitations and unresolved issues can be found in Robert Steinbrook and Bernard Lo, "Decision Making for Incompetent Patients by Designated Proxy," *The New England Journal of Medicine* 310 (June 14, 1984): 1598–1601.

21. *Making Health Care Decisions,* Vol. 1: *Report,* p. 180.

22. *Death, Dying, and the Biological Revolution,* pp. 134–136.

23. "The Preservation of Life and Self-Preservation," *Theological Studies* 41 (June 1980): 390–396. Also found in Richard A. McCormick, *How Brave a New World?* (Garden City: Doubleday & Company, Inc., 1981), pp. 371–379.

24. *Ibid., Theological Studies,* p. 395.

25. *Making Health Care Decisions,* Vol. 1: *Report,* pp. 182–183. See also *Deciding to Forego Life-Sustaining Treatment,* pp. 127–128.

26. James Childress, *Who Should Decide?* p. 174. He says, "In general, a serial or lexical ordering of decision-makers makes sense where the patient's current or previous will cannot be known: family, physicians and other health care professionals, hospital committees, and the courts. This order is appropriate unless the patient has designated a specific decision-maker" (p. 174); cf. *Priorities in Biomedical Ethics,* pp. 47–48.

27. *Ibid.;* McCormick-Veatch, "Preservation of Life," *Theological Studies,* p. 396; President's Commission, *Making Health Care Decisions,* Vol. 1: *Report,* pp. 183–188.

28. Paul Ramsey, "Two-Step Fantastic: The Continuing Case of Brother Fox," *Theological Studies* 42 (March 1981): 133.

29. *Ethics at the Edges of Life,* pp. 151, 187.

30. Richard A. McCormick, "Moral Notes," *Theological Studies* 42 (March 1981): 108.

31. New York: Simon and Schuster, 1979.

32. New York: Simon and Schuster, 1980.

33. New York: New American Library, 1960, p. 137.

34. For limits to this "therapeutic privilege," see President's Commission, *Making Health Care Decisions*, Vol. 1: *Report*, pp. 95–96.

35. This characterization of the Hippocratic tradition finds wide support in the literature. See, for example, Robert Veatch, *Death, Dying, and the Biological Revolution*, pp. 206ff.; James Childress, *Who Should Decide?* p. 129.

36. Robert Weir, "Truthtelling in Medicine," *Perspectives in Biology and Medicine* 23 (Autumn 1980): 97.

37. *Lying: Moral Choice in Public and Private Life* (New York: Pantheon Books, 1978; Vintage Books, 1979), p. 239.

38. Veatch, *Death, Dying, and the Biological Revolution*, pp. 222–228.

39. Bok, *Lying*, p. 251. This conclusion is supported by the research findings of the President's Commission. See *Making Health Care Decisions*, Vol. 1: *Report*, pp. 75–76.

40. *Ibid.*, p. 252; Childress, *Who Should Decide?* p. 132; Veatch, *Death, Dying, and the Biological Revolution*, pp. 218–222; Weir, "Truthtelling in Medicine," *Perspectives in Biology and Medicine* 23 (Autumn 1980): 108.

41. Bok, *Lying*, p. 252.

42. "The Function of Medicine," *The Hastings Center Report* 7 (December 1977): 18.

43. These substantive issues of informed consent are explained by the President's Commission, *Making Health Care Decisions*, Vol. 1: *Report*, pp. 74–85.

44. Warren T. Reich, "Towards a Theory of Autonomy and Informed Consent," *The Annual of the Society of Christian Ethics* (1982): 191–215; see esp. pp. 195–202.

45. President's Commission, *Making Health Care Decisions*, pp. 2, 38.

46. "Principles for Moral Decisions About Prolonging Life," in *Moral Responsibility in Prolonging Life Decisions*, p. 120.

47. *The Patient as Person* (New Haven: Yale University Press, 1970), p. 10.

48. On the "reasonable patient" standard in ethics and law, see President's Commission, *Making Health Care Decisions*, Vol. 1: *Report*, p. 103.

49. On the mode of presentation of information, see *ibid.,* pp. 89–93; see also Childress, *Who Should Decide?* pp. 134–135.

50. Donald Oken, "What To Tell Cancer Patients: A Study of Medical Attitudes," *JAMA* 175 (April 1, 1961): 1120–1128.

51. Dennis H. Novack, *et al.,* "Changes in Physicians' Attitudes Toward Telling the Cancer Patient," *JAMA* 241 (March 2, 1979): 897–900.

52. Robert M. Veatch and Ernest Tai, "Talking About Death: Patterns of Lay and Professional Change," *The Annals of the American Academy of Political and Social Science* 447 (January 1980): 36–45.

53. For these two moral perspectives, see Childress, *Who Should Decide?* p. 145, and Veatch, *Death, Dying, and the Biological Revolution,* p. 239.

54. Weir, "Truthtelling in Medicine," *Perspectives in Biology and Medicine* 23 (Autumn 1980): 108.

55. President's Commission, *Making Health Care Decisions,* Vol. 1: *Report,* pp. 93–96.

56. Veatch, *Death, Dying, and the Biological Revolution,* p. 244. Childress agrees with this position; see *Who Should Decide?* pp. 150–151.

57. Veatch, *Death, Dying, and the Biological Revolution,* p. 245.

58. *Ibid.,* p. 246.

59. Childress, *Who Should Decide?* p. 148.

60. Veatch, *Death, Dying, and the Biological Revolution,* pp. 247–248.

61. "Telling Patients," in Stanley J. Reiser, Arthur J. Dyck and William J. Curran, editors, *Ethics in Medicine: Historical Perspectives and Contemporary Concerns* (Cambridge: The MIT Press, 1977), p. 238.

62. *Questions and Answers on Death and Dying* (New York: Macmillan Publishing Co., Collier Books, 1974), p. 3.

63. The literature on the hospice movement is rapidly growing. Two good introductory works are Paul M. DuBois, *The Hospice Way of Death* (New York: Human Sciences Press, 1980), and Anne Munley, *The Hospice Alternative* (New York: Basic Books, Inc., 1983). A serviceable resource for the general population in lay language on how hospice works and what can be expected of it is Kenneth B. Wentzel, *To Those Who Need It Most, Hospice Means Hope* (Boston: Charles River Books, 1981). Two brief articles on the experience of hospice in America are David H. Smith and Judith A. Granbois, "The American Way of Hospice," *The Hastings Center Report* 12 (April 1982): 8–10, and, Peter Mudd, "High

Ideals and Hard Cases: The Evolution of a Hospice," *The Hastings Center Report* 12 (April 1982): 11–14.

64. As quoted in Robert F. Rizzo, "Hospice: Comprehensive Terminal Care," *New York State Journal of Medicine* 78 (October 1978): 1902.

65. For brief comments on each of these principles by a hospice physician, see Robert F. Twycross, "Debate: Euthanasia—A Physician's Viewpoint," *Journal of Medical Ethics* 8 (June 1982): 88–90.

66. Present hospice legislation in the U.S., due to expire on January 1, 1986, allows medicare reimbursement for a maximum of two benefit periods of ninety days each and one period of thirty days. The economic issues related to the hospice movement in America and related legislative efforts to secure federal funding are reviewed in Munley, *The Hospice Alternative,* pp. 281–293.

67. John F. Potter lists other challenges facing the hospice movement to be the quality of care given, the quality of the care-givers, the practice of controlling pain with narcotics and the danger of drug abuse, financial concerns, and using hospice to do research on pain-control. See "A Challenge for the Hospice Movement," *The New England Journal of Medicine* 302 (January 3, 1980): 53–55. For a positive evaluation of the advantages hospice can bring to the health care delivery system, see Robert F. Rizzo, "Hospice: Comprehensive Terminal Care," *New York State Journal of Medicine,* esp. pp. 1906–1909.

68. Munley, *The Hospice Alternative,* pp. 32–33.

69. DuBois, *The Hospice Way of Death,* p. 74.

70. The Brompton mixture is the analgesic widely used at St. Christopher's Hospice. As Dubois reports, "it is an oral mixture consisting of 2.5 mg (or more) of heroin, 10 mg of cocaine, 2.5 ml of ethyl alcohol (95 percent), and 5 ml of syrup (66 percent sucrose in water) made up to 20 ml by addition of chloroform water. Almost all patients receive a phenothiazine syrup with the diamorphine mixture, to relieve coexistent nausea or vomiting as well as to mask the bitter taste of the diamorphine." (*The Hospice Way of Death,* p. 71). At the Connecticut Hospice, Inc., pain relief is a mixture of morphine and water (ibid., p. 99). Cecily Saunders reports that morphine is used in the majority of doses of an oral analgesic at St. Christopher's Hospice and that diamorphine (heroin) remains the drug of choice for subcutaneous injection. She wants to correct the false notion that hospice care equals heroin. She says, "The quite widespread belief that hospice care equals heroin or even the Brompton mixture is inaccurate and may well harm the hospice move-

ment itself." See her "Hospice Care," *The American Journal of Medicine* 65 (November 1978): 727.

71. Saunders, *ibid.*.

72. See Rizzo, "Hospice: Comprehensive Terminal Care," *New York State Journal of Medicine,* p. 1904.

Chapter 5
The Moral Art of Terminal Care

1. See, for example, the last chapter in Tom L. Beauchamp and James F. Childress, *Principles of Biomedical Ethics,* Second Edition (New York: Oxford University Press, 1983), pp. 255–280.

2. Stanley Hauerwas, "Medicine as a Tragic Profession," with Richard Bondi and David B. Burrell, *Truthfulness and Tragedy* (Notre Dame: University of Notre Dame Press, 1977), p. 186.

3. New York: Ballantine Books, 1972, p. 150.

4. For a theological analysis of the relation of our beliefs about God and our moral perspectives, attitudes and intentions, see James M. Gustafson, *The Contributions of Theology to Medical Ethics* (Milwaukee: Marquette University Theology Department, 1975).

5. For an analysis of the relation of our belief in immortality and moral responsibility, see Marjorie Reiley Maguire, "Ethics and Immortality," *The American Society of Christian Ethics: 1978 Selected Papers,* ed. Max L. Stackhouse (Waterloo, Ontario: Council on the Study of Religion, 1978), pp. 42–61. For an interpretation of the doctrine of eternal life and implications for care for the dying, see Hans Küng, *Eternal Life? Life After Death as a Medical, Philosophical, and Theological Problem,* trans. Edward Quinn (Garden City: Doubleday & Company, Inc., 1984), esp. pp. 149–175.

6. For an analysis of the impact of these forces on health care, see Richard A. McCormick, "Bioethical Issues and the Moral Matrix of U.S. Health Care," *Hospital Progress* 60 (May 1979): 42–45.

7. For a model of practitioner-patient relationships which tries to achieve this balance, see the President's Commission's Report, *Making Health Care Decisions* (Washington: U.S. Government Printing Office, 1982), pp. 36–39; also, Robert M. Veatch, "Models for Ethical Medicine in a Revolutionary Age," *Hastings Center Report* 2 (June 1972): 5–7; also, Robert M. Veatch, *A Theory of Medical Ethics* (New York: Basic Books, Inc., 1981), pp. 108–138.

8. President's Commission, *Deciding to Forego Life-Sustaining Treatment* (Washington: U.S. Government Printing Office, 1983), p. 76.

For an analysis of the moral significance of the withholding/withdrawing distinction, see pp. 73–77.

9. Benedict Ashley, "Principles for Moral Decisions About Prolonging Life," in *Moral Responsibility in Prolonging Life Decisions,* edited by Donald G. McCarthy and Albert Moraczewski (St. Louis: Pope John Center, 1981), p. 121.

10. Paul Ramsey, *The Patient as Person* (New Haven: Yale University Press, 1970), p. 151.

11. For a consideration of some measures appropriate for comfort, see President's Commission, *Deciding to Forego Life-Sustaining Treatment,* Appendix B, pp. 275–297.

Selected Readings

The literature on euthanasia and its related issues is enormous. Much of this literature has appeared in article form rather than in full length books. As a result, many anthologies have been compiled to bring together significant articles related to death and dying issues. The readings cited in the "Notes" at the end of this book, as well as those suggested here, represent only a small part of the vast material available on this subject.

Issues pertaining to the determination of death are well presented in the report of the President's Commission, *Defining Death* (Washington: U.S. Government Printing Office, 1981). The Catholic Health Association has published a small pamphlet on theological, medical, ethical and legal issues pertaining to this issue in *Determination of Death,* edited by Albert S. Moraczewski and J. Stuart Showalter (St. Louis: Catholic Health Association, 1982). Douglas N. Walton, *Brain Death: Ethical Considerations* (West Lafayette: Purdue University Press, 1980) provides another short treatment of pertinent issues. Robert Veatch has summarized well the issues pertaining to the determining of death issue in his two chapters "Defining Death Anew: Technical and Ethical Problems" and "Defining Death Anew: Policy Options," in *Death, Dying, and the Biological Revolution* (New Haven: Yale University Press, 1976), pp. 21–76. Paul Ramsey has also provided his perspective on these issues in his chapter "On Updating Procedures for Stating That a Man Has Died" in *The Patient as Person* (New Haven: Yale University Press, 1970), pp. 59–112.

Underlying theological and philosophical issues relevant to the euthanasia discussion and principles pertaining to care for the dying are discussed in two reports of the President's Commission, *Deciding to Forego Life-Sustaining Treatment* (Washington: U.S. Government Printing Office, 1983) and *Making Health Care Decisions* Vol. 1 (Washington: U.S. Government Printing Office, 1982). James M. Childress has provided a thorough study of the dimensions of the issue "Who decides?" in his work, *Who Should Decide?* (New York: Oxford University Press, 1982). Robert Veatch has also explored the issues and principles involved in euthanasia and care for the dying in his masterful work, *Death, Dying, and the Biological Revolution* (New Haven: Yale University Press, 1976).

The articles and books indicated in the "Notes" of Chapter Three provide sufficient references for further reading of those whose positions are represented in that chapter. One book continues to be a helpful study of teleological and deontological approaches to issues in medical ethics: Tom L. Beauchamp and James F. Childress, *Principles of Biomedical Ethics* (New York: Oxford University Press, 1979).

Several anthologies provide articles pertaining to the issues and principles underlying the euthanasia discussions. Three of them are Tom L. Beauchamp and Seymour Perlin, eds., *Ethical Issues in Death and Dying* (Englewood Cliffs: Prentice-Hall, Inc., 1978); Robert F. Weir, ed., *Ethical Issues in Death and Dying* (New York: Columbia University Press, 1977); Dennis J. Horan and David Mall, eds., *Death, Dying, and Euthanasia* (Frederick, MD: University Publications of America, Inc., 1980).

No single volume satisfactorily addresses the moral art of caring for the terminally ill. However, two books do provide important perspectives on this issue: Donald G. McCarthy and Albert S. Moraczewski, eds., *Moral Responsibility in Prolonging Life Decisions* (St. Louis: Pope John Center, 1981), and Albert R. Jonsen, Mark Siegler and William J. Winslade, *Clinical Ethics* (New York: Macmillan Publishing Co., Inc., 1982).

What are they saying about Mysticism? *by Harvey D. Egan, S.J.*
What are they saying about Christ and World Religions?
    by Lucien Richard, O.M.I.
What are they saying about non-Christian Faith?
    by Denise Lardner Carmody
What are they saying about Christian-Jewish Relations?
    by John T. Pawlikowski
What are they saying about Creation? *by Zachary Hayes, O.F.M.*
What are they saying about the Prophets? *by David P. Reid, SS.CC.*
What are they saying about Moral Norms? *by Richard M. Gula, S.S.*
What are they saying about Death and Christian Hope?
    by Monika Hellwig
What are they saying about Sexual Morality? *by James P. Hanigan*
What are they saying about Jesus? *by Gerald O'Collins*
What are they saying about Dogma? *by William E. Reiser, S.J.*
What are they saying about Peace and War? *by Thomas A. Shannon*
What are they saying about Papal Primacy?
    by J. Michael Miller, C.S.B.
What are they saying about Matthew? *by Donald Senior, C.P.*
What are they saying about the End of the World?
    by Zachary Hayes, O.F.M.
What are they saying about the Grace of Christ?
    by Brian O. McDermott, S.J.
What are they saying about Wisdom Literature?
    by Dianne Bergant, C.S.A.
What are they saying about Biblical Archaeology?
    by Leslie J. Hoppe, O.F.M.
What are they saying about Mary? *by Anthony J. Tambasco*
What are they saying about Scripture and Ethics?
    by William C. Spohn, S.J.
What are they saying about the Social Setting of the New Testament?
    by Carolyn Osiek, R.S.C.J.
What are they saying about Theological Method?
    by J.J. Mueller, S.J.
What are they saying about Virtue? *by Anthony J. Tambasco*
What are they saying about Genetic Engineering?
    by Thomas A. Shannon
What are they saying about Paul? *by Joseph Plevnik, S.J.*
What are they saying about Salvation? *by Rev. Denis Edwards*